Roadmap to

Roadmap to Renewal

Rediscovering the Church's Mission

REVISED EDITION
WITH STUDY GUIDE

Douglas Ruffle

CASCADE *Books* · Eugene, Oregon

ROADMAP TO RENEWAL
Rediscovering the Church's Mission, Revised Edition with Study Guide

Cascade Books
An Imprint of Wipf and Stock Publishers
199 W. 8th Ave., Suite 3
Eugene, OR 97401

www.wipfandstock.com

PAPERBACK ISBN: 978-1-4982-9721-9
HARDCOVER ISBN: 978-1-4982-9723-3
EBOOK ISBN: 978-1-4982-9722-6

Cataloging-in-Publication data:

Names: Ruffle, Douglas
Title: Roadmap to renewal : rediscovering the church's mission, revised edition with study guide / by Douglas Ruffle.
Description: Eugene, OR : Cascade Books, 2017 | Includes bibliographical references.
Identifiers: ISBN 978-1-4982-9721-9 (paperback) | ISBN 978-1-4982-9723-3 (hardcover) | ISBN 978-1-4982-9722-6 (ebook)
Subjects: LCSH: Church renewal—United Methodist Church (U.S.) | Mission of the church.
Classification: LCC BX8382.2.Z5 R84 2017 (print) | LCC BX8382.2.Z5

Manufactured in the U.S.A.

To my loving wife,
Tammie Ruffle

Contents

Acknowledgments ix

Welcome 1

Introduction: Readiness 5

1. Reality Check 17

2. Reconnect 29

3. Rediscover the Landscape of Our Parish 41

4. Reassess Our Current Ministry 50

5. Road Break 62

6. Reaching Younger People 70

7. Roadmaps Start with Vision 79

8. Realign Mission, Goals, and Objectives 89

9. Roadmarkers on the Road to Renewal 99

Study Guide 105

Bibliography 133

Acknowledgments

I GIVE THANKS FOR the opportunity to have served as Team Coordinator of Congregational Development for the Greater New Jersey Annual Conference from 2003–2013. Much of what is written here is the fruit of learning from visits to churches in this conference. I give thanks to God for these churches and the interaction we have had over the years.

Portions of this book were first published as part of a regular column called "Vital Congregations," in the *Relay*, a publication of the Greater New Jersey Annual Conference. I thank the editor of the *Relay*, the Reverend Robin Van Cleef, for his helpful input and constant encouragement.

Other portions first appeared in the *Discovery Church Journey: An Invitation to Congregational Transformation*, published by the General Board of Global Ministries (2002). I am grateful to the Reverend Robert Harman, a former colleague at Global Ministries, for his support and encouragement.

I am indebted to Dr. Robert E. "Bob" Logan for his mentorship and coaching. His writings have helped deepen my thinking on the theme of Journey as I wrestled with the analogy of the road trip. Bob has also been a central part of the Natural Church Development (NCD) movement in the United States. I have learned much from NCD and have incorporated insights into this book. Bob also read the manuscript of this book and gave helpful and encouraging feedback.

I am deeply grateful to the late Reverend Dr. Douglas W. Johnson for his insightful comments and editorial improvements to this manuscript. Dr. Johnson served as Director of Research at the General Board of Global Ministries and was a valuable mentor in congregational development to me and many others. A circle of readers read the first draft of the manuscript and gave helpful comments and needed corrections. Thank you Jack and Joslin Ruffle (my brother and sister-in-law), Jack Scharf, Marcelle Dotson, Bishop Sudarshana Devadhar, Varlyna Wright, and my wife, Tammie Ruffle, without whose support and encouragement this book would never have come to light. Their feedback has made this a better book. Thank you!

Welcome

THE GOSPEL OF JOHN records a story of a man who was sick for thirty-eight years awaiting healing by a pool. At the time of a festival, Jesus was on his way to Jerusalem when he passed by the pool around which the "blind, lame, and paralyzed" (John 5:3) awaited the time when the waters of the pool were stirred and a miraculous healing by angels would cure those who entered it at the right time. Jesus was made aware that the man had been lying by this pool for a long, long time. Now in other biblical stories of healing, often it is the one in need who catches Jesus' attention. In this passage, however, Jesus speaks first. He asks a simple question: "Do you want to be made well?" (John 5:6b).

It is a logical question. The sick man had been there for nearly four decades and still was in need of being well. If it had taken this long, maybe he didn't really want to be healed? In response to Jesus' question, the sick man begins to give excuses for being in this condition. "I have no one to put me into the pool when the water is stirred up; and while I am making my way, someone else steps down ahead of me" (John 5:7).

Jesus then commands him to "stand up, take your mat and walk." The biblical account says all of this happened on the Sabbath, which makes it a story about proper observance of the fourth commandment. In a time like ours in the life of the church, however, I keep returning to the incident with the sick man as a parable that speaks to those churches today that have been "lying around" for many years, waiting for things to get better, as if

1

some miraculous turn of events can reverse the decline they are experiencing. I want to say to them, "You mean in all these years you could not come up with a plan?" Instead of excuses, what if the sick man sought the help of others so that he could enter into the pool at the proper time? In the case of many churches I have visited and known, couldn't they find help from others to come up with a plan that would help them become more vital, more active in their communities and more inviting to the growing numbers of people who no longer find meaning in being part of a church?

This book was written to provide a roadmap toward wellness. It was written to lay out a process by which church leaders—lay and clergy—could come up with their own roadmap that would become their plan of action over the next several years to become well, healthy and inviting to people not yet a part of their congregation. Over the years since the first edition of this book was published in 2009, I have received completed "roadmaps" from churches that have gone on a journey together to come up with a plan. This new edition will include some of those plans and discoveries. This new edition of the book also includes a study guide as an appendix to the text so that a team or class in a church can follow its map. Many of the plans made by churches that have followed the process laid out in this book produced fruit that manifested itself in reaching more people, younger people and more diverse people from their community. The journey takes patience and persistence and holds the promise of bringing new life and vitality for your community of faith. It's like going on a road trip with a bunch of friends and discovering new sights together about the very community you have lived in for years and years.

I don't know about you, but I love going on trips. As a child we traveled by car. Sometimes we went far away as when we drove from New York to San Francisco and back. Most of the times, we visited friends for a weekend in a neighboring state. There was always excitement and adventure as we discovered new places and learned new things about our world. Later in life I experienced the excitement of long-distance bus trips and train rides. On those occasions I tried to get a window seat to see the landscape as we passed by areas of the world I had never seen before.

Roadmap to Renewal is a book that invites you to go on a road trip to rediscover the mission and purpose of your church. Be prepared to learn new things along the way about your world and the mission to which God has called you. The book invites you to open your minds and hearts to what God is calling your church to be and do.

Some of my fondest memories of trips taken came at the onset when the idea itself was new. We would take out our maps and imagine what it would be like to go to new places. I invite you to look through the contents of this book even before you begin its journey. Read several of the questions at the end of chapters to see what will be asked of you along the way. Imagine what it will be like to take a journey with other brothers and sisters of the church to a new destination. My prayer is that you embrace the trip as an adventure that will help you rediscover ministry and mission in exciting ways.

Introduction

Readiness

GOD'S PEOPLE TRAVEL. ABRAHAM and Sarah journeyed from Ur to Haran and from Haran to Canaan (Gen 11:31—12:5). Moses led the people of Israel out of Egypt toward the promised land, a journey full of danger and challenges as they crossed the Red Sea and wandered through the wilderness. That journey, described in the Old Testament, was full of trials and missteps, faithfulness and apostasy, revelation and rebellion.

Joseph and Mary traveled the road from Nazareth to Bethlehem for the birth of Jesus. After his birth, they detoured so that they went through Egypt on their way back to Nazareth. They had received a divine message that they ran the risk of being victims of violence unless they embarked on a migrant journey.

Saul met Christ on the road to Damascus. After that dramatic confrontation, he quit persecuting followers of the Way, changed his name to Paul, and became the most important apostle in the early church.

In many Bible stories, God's promises were fulfilled at the end of a journey. During their journey, they confronted difficulties and disappointments, and, as a people, learned new ways of living. They also discovered how better to approach and listen to God.

An example of this was Cleopas and another disciple who were returning from Jerusalem on the road to Emmaus (Luke 24:13–35) after Jesus' trial and crucifixion. As they were traveling, the resurrected Jesus met them on the road. The story tells us Jesus appeared to them as a stranger; he walked with them, but "their eyes were kept from recognizing him" (24:16).

Think what might have happened if he had said, "Hey, it's me, Jesus; can't you see I've risen from the dead?" Jesus related to them differently. He led them to discover his presence. He asked, "What are you discussing with each other while you walk along?" (Luke 24:17).

Cleopas stopped and said, "Are you the only stranger in Jerusalem who does not know the things that have taken place there in these days?" (24:18). He might have said, "Are you so blind that you don't know what has happened?" Cleopas answered the stranger's question with hostility.

Churches that have experienced a decline may have the same feeling as Cleopas. They cannot believe a stranger cannot see that they have been losing members. Many church members may react with hostility to the suggestion that they need to start on a road to renewal. Other churches may be jaded because they have made too many attempts at renewal. They can testify that they have had no success in following the latest "grand new idea" that was guaranteed to turn things around. Throughout his ministry, Christ tried to lead people to the living waters of faith that flow to God through him. People who have been down have a hard time seeing hope, even when it is staring them in the face.

As we follow the story of Cleopas and the other disciple, we find guidance for a journey of hope. Jesus showed us how to approach the skeptical, the reluctant and those who have given up hope. In his encounter with the two disciples on the Emmaus Road, he asked questions that engaged them in dialogue. That dialogue led them to discovery.

Jesus asked, "What things [have gone on in Jerusalem]?" They told him that Jesus had been a mighty prophet. His body was no longer in the tomb and some women had claimed to have seen angels who said he was alive.

Jesus listened as they said, "We had hoped." Their hope was now gone.

Jesus asked, "Was it not necessary that the Messiah should suffer these things and then enter into his glory?" (Luke 24:26). He reminded them of the Scriptures. He explained how everything that happened had been laid out in the Bible from the time of Moses through the prophets.

Later, they remarked, "Were not our hearts burning within us while he was talking to us on the road, while he was opening the scriptures to us?" (Luke 24:32).

Jesus knew how to respond to their situation because he listened to them, asked questions, and responded with the Word. Jesus didn't intrude. When they arrived at the village, "he walked ahead as if he were going on. But they urged him strongly, saying, 'Stay with us, because it is almost evening and the day is now nearly over'" (Luke 24:28–29). He was no longer a stranger. He was a friend and they invited him into their home.

Jesus had provided the opportunity for them to discover him. Jesus had listened and had responded to their despair. He had been a stranger on the road, an unknown man. They talked with Jesus and each other until his strangeness dissolved into friendship. Jesus went in with them, and "when he was at the table with them, he took bread, blessed and broke it, and gave it to them" (Luke 24:30). When he broke bread with them, "Their eyes were opened, and they recognized him" (Luke 24:31).

Why would regaining hope, and a vision of mission, be different for the people of a local church? We embark on a journey together to find the fulfillment of God's promises for our lives and our communities. We find our way by traveling the road together. Sometimes a church finds itself off track, sometimes the members are despondent. These churches are on their road to Emmaus. They know the story of Jesus but their walk is listless. Their faith lacks passion. They need someone to listen and ask questions. They want to rediscover the burning in their hearts that gives meaning to their mission as people of God. The gospel invites us to work our way back so that we can find the pathway forward. The blessing for Cleopas and the other disciple came at the end of their road trip, when at last they recognized Christ in the breaking of the bread.

Before the days of GPS, computerized directions and cell phones, I had to rely on my ability to interpret a map. Once, I got lost in a rural area of Iowa. It was nighttime. I had gotten off track on my way from a church to a hotel. Driving along in the dark, suddenly I was on an unpaved road hemmed in by tall corn stalks on both sides. How would I find my way out of this maze?

I put my emergency blinkers on and stopped the car. The map I had brought along was of no use. I had no idea where I was and no compass to tell in which direction I was headed. The needle indicated fuel was dipping below a quarter of a tank.

As I sat in the car with the windows down, only the sound of crickets and flying insects filled the air. Nearly 10 p.m., tired from a long day of meetings and workshops, I longed to get into the hotel room and rest. I wondered if I dared stop at a farmhouse and plead for help to get me on my way.

I was desperate enough to try. I started the car and drove until I found a house with lights on. I rang the doorbell. A light went on in the front porch where I stood and a tall man greeted me at the door. With map in hand, I said, "Hi. I'm lost."

I told him where I hoped to go. He smiled, pointed out on the map where we were, and said, "You are about two miles from that hotel." He told me how to get there. "I am so grateful," I said as I turned to leave.

Have you ever been so lost that you didn't even know how lost you were? That was me, a New Yorker in rural Iowa. It was similar to when I arrived as the new pastor of a church that had nowhere to go but up. In both cases, I needed help finding my way forward. I needed someone to come alongside me, like Jesus, to show me the promise of Scripture and the hope he brings to us.

My prayer is that *Roadmap to Renewal* will provide the guidance you need to learn where you are currently and help you arrive at the destination God desires for your church. You may not sense that you are lost right now. You may have a good idea of where you are; but, you may not be happy with your current situation. Every church, even healthy and fast-growing ones, can benefit from an experience of discovery that takes them to the next level of vitality and growth.

Many churches wonder if they are on the right road. Many churches sense that they need a new roadmap to lead them to a more God-directed, Spirit-infused place, where ministry and mission are healthy and alive. This book is offered as a roadmap to help your church journey toward a new sense of mission and ministry in the always challenging terrain of being the church in the twenty-first century.

Getting Ready

The first step for any journey is "getting ready." What do we need to prepare for the journey?

We must *want* to take the trip. Starting on a journey of discovering what God wants your church to be and do, begins with a sense of urgency that there can be a better way to do ministry. The primary issue at the start of a journey is an assessment of whether or not you want to leave home. Some churches that would rather not change live on memories of when the church thrived, attendance was stronger, and bills could be paid more easily. They prefer to preserve those memories. In many ways their mission as a church looks more like the purpose of a museum than that of a thriving mission outpost.

For twenty years, a church in a major New Jersey city had lived off of the generosity of previous generations who left money to their beloved church in their wills. During those twenty years, changes took place in the neighborhood. People who attended the church commuted from their homes which were outside the city. A growing disconnect separated the church from the neighborhood as members drove late model vehicles for Sunday morning worship into a section of the city where people struggled to meet the basics of survival.

As the funds from their endowment were dwindling, it was becoming clear that unless the church changed its ways, it would not survive. The demographic profile of the neighborhood no longer matched the profile of the church membership.

During our conversations about possible ways the church could reengage with the neighborhood, it became clear that the members had little desire to do so. One member expressed the sentiment of the dozen or more members when she said, "Let's just spend down the money until there isn't any left." She was asking them not to change a thing about the church or its mission. She did not want them to take a journey that would lead to change.

Any church can turn its situation around when it changes from an inward to an outward focus. On the other hand, it is better for a church to be honest about its refusal to leave home than to embark on a journey half-heartedly. This New Jersey city church lasted about two more years and then decided to close. The good news is that the building was sold and the assets used to start a new ministry in the same city. Sometimes a church needs to die in order for new life and new ministry to emerge.

Before setting out on the road to renewal a church must be honest enough to decide if it wants to make the journey. As the church prays about this, it should consider the pros and cons of taking the journey. What might happen should it decide to engage in a process of renewal? What might happen if it decides to stay at home and keep things as they are for as long as possible?

I encourage church leadership not to wallow in blame or guilt should they decide not to get involved with a process of renewal. They are the faithful remnant of saints who have kept the doors of their church open. In most cases, the decline of the church came about due to circumstances beyond their control. There are many factors that contributed to the present state of the church. Deciding not to travel the road to renewal can be a choice to die with dignity. Jesus said that "unless a grain of wheat falls into the earth and dies, it remains just a single grain; but if it dies, it bears much fruit" (John 12:24).

For a church to die with dignity, it needs to consider how to allow its legacy to bear fruit for making disciples. While the city church cited above was honest about its inability to reengage ministry in its neighborhood, it could have decided to leverage what resources it had left while these could make a larger difference. Rather than spend down their endowment until it was all gone, they could have offered it along with their building to the broader church to sow the seeds for making new disciples. Making a decision to die with dignity is a mature and self-giving decision.

Most churches that consider the road to renewal will not be in such dire straits that the decision is life or death. All churches regardless of the state of their present vitality would do well to engage in a process that assesses their mission and ministry. It is always the right time to fulfill the promise of being a God-centered, mission-oriented, church.

The first question a church must ask itself is whether or not it wants to embark on a journey of renewal. Is it willing to invest the time and effort to venture forward?

Some years ago, churches across the United States were invited to take a journey through a workbook published by the General Board of Global Ministries (GBGM). The workbook, *The Discovery Church Journey: An Invitation to Congregational Transformation*, was used by churches throughout the connection. When supplies of the resource were running out, GBGM seized the opportunity to rewrite it to include insights and feedback that participating churches had given. *Roadmap to Renewal*, while drawing on some of the information in the original workbook, is a new resource that draws upon the lessons learned from *The Discovery Church Journey*.

Since writing *The Discovery Church Journey*, my thinking on the subject of congregational transformation has been enriched by others writing in the field. Robert E. Logan and Tara Miller wrote an excellent book that has influenced me. In *From Followers to Leaders*, they draw the analogy of a coach coming alongside a person for a trail hike. The "path" has parallels to the notion of the road trip. I am deeply indebted to their work.

Other insights gained from the Natural Church Development movement have worked their way into my thoughts and writing. I am grateful to ChurchSmart Resources and their publisher, Dave

Wetzler, for many of the concepts I have come to incorporate into my own thinking and vocabulary.

There are no quick fixes that will transform churches from a declining institution into an expanding, robust and active church. Churches that become renewed use a lot of prayer, revisioning and redirection. It takes time. The only way it happens is through patience, persistence, and following a process. The *Roadmap* outlines a process that will help guide your church from where it is to the preferred future God envisions for you.

Selecting a Leadership Team

Once the church leadership decides to set out on the road to renewal, other preparations must be made. Make sure that the governing council of the church is on board by giving their approval of the venture. Enlist the support of the entire church in the decision to embark on the road to renewal. Gaining ownership on the part of the church body from the beginning will help the process go forward.

Recruiting a good leadership team is vital to the success of church renewal. Select people with skills in problem-solving and creative thinking, and who have the ability to plan. Include persons with these talents on the team even if they are not core members of the church.

Recruit the chair of the team first. While the pastor plays a key role in the journey, I recommend that the leadership team be led by a layperson. This person should have good listening skills and be able to lead a team. Consider inviting at least one person to join the team who is from the community and who is not a member of the church. This person might be the spouse of an active member who attends another church (or attends no church at all). Such an individual brings fresh eyes and ears to the task.

The size of the team should be small enough to ensure group communication and large enough to represent the size of the congregation. A small-membership church could have as few as six persons and a large-membership church as many as fifteen. They should be given a status that will enable them to influence the congregation and to follow through on the implementation of the process. Avoid assigning a current standing committee with the task of serving as the leadership team.

At First United Methodist Church, Chula Vista, California, the nominations committee took special care to gather a team that was representative of the congregation's diversity in age, race, educational background and length of membership. Nine persons were chosen.

As the team is selected, communicate expectations of team membership clearly. Be clear about how often the team will meet and for what duration. Map out a schedule of meetings. Consider drafting a covenant that each member of the leadership team signs as a symbol of the commitment being made to the journey.[1]

Consecrate the team by inviting them to come forward at a worship service and having the pastor and lay leader lay hands on them. In this way the entire congregation is aware of the road to renewal and the people who are embarking on the journey on behalf of the entire church.

As the journey unfolds, remind people on the leadership team of the promises they made. Life often gets in the way of the best of plans so there may be people who need to leave the team. When that happens, others can be invited to join. You want to aim for consistently strong attendance at meetings, and you want people to fulfill their assignments between meetings.

Communicate with the congregation frequently. It is vital that everyone in the congregation is aware of the discoveries made by the team. Periodic reports to the congregation via online bulletins, church newsletters, and worship "mission moments" will keep persons updated.

1. Go to http://www.dougruffle.com/roadmap-to-renewal-information/ for sample covenants for leadership teams.

What Kind of GPS System Will You Use for This Journey?

Once you have your leader and team members selected, and you have outlined expectations, distribute copies of this book to everyone on the team. Have them read this introduction in anticipation of the first meeting. During that meeting review the content of the introduction and then answer the questions under "Your Turn" together. Have someone record notes so that the insights and information gathered at each session can serve as reference for future meetings. Treat the book as you would the curriculum for an adult Bible study.

The exercises in the "Your Turn" section at the end of each chapter are the travel segments for your roadmap. They build on each other. In the appendix there is a Study Guide that provides an agenda for a local church team to follow a step-by-step process in building the elements of a plan. By the time the team finishes the book, you should have a roadmap to renewal that reflects the context of your church. The journey itself serves as the process to rediscover the church's mission.

Decide whether or not you want to employ the services of a coach. While the analogy does not always hold true, a coach can be like a GPS system as you travel on the roadway to renewal. GPS stands for "global positioning system." It provides navigation via satellite so that cars can stay on track toward their destination. For our purposes, it stands for "Guided Process Servant"—a coach who can guide the roadmap to renewal process. Just like a car's GPS, your team is responsible for making the turns, steering the way ahead.

The GPS system is only as good as your ability to follow its directions (or respond to the questions). A good coach (a Guided Process Servant) can serve this function by asking questions that dig deep into the collective consciousness of the team. Your denominational leadership should be able to help you identify qualified coaches. You can also seek help through the services of CoachNet International (http://www.coachnet.org).

Your Turn

1. Is there a sense of urgency to set out on a road to renewal? Do you feel the need to reassess the direction of your mission? Why? What's at stake? What will happen if you don't? What may happen if you do?

2. Review together the story of the road to Emmaus (Luke 24:13–35). How does Jesus' encounter with the two disciples show us a way toward renewal?

3. Are clergy and lay leadership of the church committed to take an honest look at the church's mission and direction? What do you need to do to gain more support to rediscover the church's mission?

4. Is there a team of people from the church willing to commit to this process by attending meetings and completing assignments between sessions?

5. Can you participate in the process yourselves or do you need help from an outside coach (Guided Process Servant)?

1

Reality Check

WHEN A CHURCH DECIDES to embark on a journey of renewal, it needs to begin with a review of where it is now. It asks, "What is our current reality?"

A church needs to know the criteria by which congregational health is measured. Many denominations measure effectiveness by counting how many members they have, what the annual budget is, whether or not it can pay into the apportionment system, and how many are enrolled in Sunday School. While the "numbers game" may not take the most complete picture of effective ministry, it should not be dismissed either. Luke mentions the number of believers added to the followers of Jesus on several occasions in the Acts of the Apostles. "So those who welcomed his message were baptized, and that day about three thousand persons were added" (Acts 2:41).

In the context of North American culture, it is difficult to measure effectiveness apart from counting heads and offering plate receipts. It is part of our current reality.

Another component of reality is to research where we were ten years ago and compare it with where we are now. Compare average worship attendance, membership, Sunday school enrollment and ability to pay into the apportionment system of the denomination then and now.

There are other ways to measure effectiveness in ministry. How many people have joined our church by profession of faith (as opposed to transfer)? How many persons are participating in mission programs? How many missionaries are we sending into the community to volunteer at soup kitchens, food pantries, or homeless shelters?

The leadership team should decide what scorecard it will use to measure effectiveness in ministry. A scorecard measures progress by agreed-upon benchmarks. When going to a baseball game, we use a scorecard to record hits, runs, and errors. At the end of the ballgame we see how each individual performed and we gain a picture of the overall performance of the team. Whether we call it a scorecard or not, each denomination uses a set of criteria to measure the effectiveness of a church.

The idea behind a "reality check" is to assess the current situation of the church. How healthy of a congregation are we today? There are several assessment tools a church could use to take an honest look at itself, such as the Natural Church Development survey or Readiness 360.[1] I invite you to measure your church in light of the central focus of Jesus' teaching: the reign of God. Ask your church how it aligns with being a sign, preview, and instrument of God's reign.

God's strategic plan for humankind is that the reign of God pervade the hearts and minds of the people of the earth. Jesus' central message was to proclaim this reign of God and to invite hearers to enter it.

Georgia Harkness, a twentieth-century seminary professor and author of very readable books on theology and spirituality, defined the reign of God in this way: "It is the righteous, loving rule of God."[2] It is a realm where the love and justice of God prevail. It is something that is already here because of the ministry of Jesus and yet it is still to come because the whole world does not live the way Jesus would have us live.

---

1. See http://readiness360.org/ for more information.
2. Harkness, *Understanding the Christian Faith*, 159.

The late James W. Fowler, who served as a professor at Candler School of Theology in Atlanta, Georgia, describes the reign of God as "God's universal commonwealth of love."[3] Others speak of it as "the blessed community of love" or "God's new society." The reign of God is a comprehensive new reality and vision where God's rule, grace, justice, and mercy are practiced. We are invited to participate in this new reality. It is both a future reality that will come when God's ultimate victory is consummated and a reality already among us that we have received as a gift.

Nowhere in the Bible does it say that the community of faith is to *build* the reign of God. We are invited to "see" it (Mark 9:1), or to "enter" it (John 3:5), to "receive" it (Mark 10:15), or "proclaim" it (Luke 9:2). We are never asked to build it. The distinction is important. If we were to build it, then it would be the work of our efforts, something *we* construct. The reign of God already exists. It is something we are invited to receive and live into.

E. Stanley Jones, a missionary to India in the twentieth century and author of twenty-nine books, including *Is the Kingdom of God Realism?*, described the reign of God as a "master conception which brings all life into integration and meaning."[4] Every aspect of life should be seen in light of the goal of living within the spiritual space of the reign of God. The reign of God should be the church's strategy, but as Jones wrote, "We have forgotten our strategy . . . and hence we are fruitlessly dealing with tactics, tinkering here and tinkering there, but it is all a vicious circle, a dog following his own tail round and round, with no goal and no meaning."[5]

The church is not to be equated with the reign of God. The reign of God is God's perfect space that humans are invited to occupy. The church is a community of imperfect people, sinners, who come together through the grace of God. The church, when it faithfully fulfills its task, serves to call the world's attention to God's reign.

3. Fowler, *Stages of Faith*, 204–11.
4. Jones, *Is the Kingdom of God Realism?*, 67.
5. Ibid., 69.

Stanley Hauerwas, the Gilbert T. Rowe Professor Emeritus of Divinity and Law at Duke Divinity School, and William Willimon, a retired bishop who now serves as Professor of the Practice of Christian Ministry at Duke, coauthored a book in 1989 that still resonates today. In *Resident Aliens*, they write, "The church was called to be a colony, an alternative community, a sign, a signal to the world that Christ has made possible a way of life together, unlike anything the world had seen."[6]

The sign in front of First United Methodist Church in Englewood, New Jersey, is perpendicular to the road so that motorists can read it as they drive by. Clean, attractive, well-lit at night, the sign always announces the times of Sunday worship and includes an encouraging phrase for passersby to read. Phrases like "God's Harvest: Forgiven People" always offer the public a word of hope grounded in Scripture.

A sign lets us know what is coming on the road ahead of us. It gives us information for our journey. A sign lets us know if we are headed in the right direction, if we are in danger, or how much longer we must travel. The church itself is called to be a "sign" of God's coming reign. It points beyond itself to the God of all creation, the God who loves, forgives, heals, creates, and seeks justice.

The church points away from itself toward God. This should be especially evident when the church gathers for worship. Christian worship is a sign the church offers to the world: there is something beyond ourselves that inspires and leads us forward. More than the physical signboard in front of our buildings, the church at worship points to the God who stands above and before us, who fills us with hope and expectation, who loves us unconditionally and offers us the grace and forgiveness to live life fully.

The image of the church as Sign was articulated by the Roman Catholic Church during Vatican II. In that historic council, which changed so much of the direction of the Roman Catholic Church, there was a paradigm shift in the understanding of the church, from the image of "sanctuary" to that of "sign."

---

6. Hauerwas and Willimon, *Resident Aliens*, 132.

Prior to Vatican II the Roman Catholic Church understood itself as a sanctuary—a sanctuary of salvation. The church was a place of refuge, protecting the faithful from the hostile environment of the world. As sanctuary, the church was a place of nurture. Vatican II preferred to speak of the church as a sign.

William Frazier, referring to this paradigm shift in 1968, likened the shift from a "sanctuary to sign" mentality as similar to shifting from an inward to an outward focus for a church. "Unlike a sanctuary," wrote Frazier, "a sign is meant to point beyond itself and to have its impact outside itself."[7] When the church embraces the image of "sign" it is open to the world, taking on an outward orientation.

Frazier distinguished "Sanctuary thinking" from "Sign thinking" in understanding the essential mission of the church. He argued that understanding the church as sanctuary "turns the Church in upon itself and away from the world and its problems."[8] The church's focus is inward, on retaining and indoctrinating members. The church emphasizes the conversion of the individual. It is the kind of emphasis that was present in Protestant churches in America, especially under the influence of its great evangelistic preachers from Charles Grandison Finney to Billy Graham. Individual salvation is the primary focus of the work of the church.

Frazier argues that a "sanctuary" church is preoccupied with numbers, but a "sign" church is much more concerned with how it lives out its relationship to the reign of God. Frazier understood the Roman Catholic Church of his day as in crisis. Many Protestants and Orthodox Christians would echo that concern today. Frazier's challenge is as true today as it was forty years ago: "Christians have not been called to the Church for their own sakes, but for the sake of others—to serve as a sign and instrument of God's universal saving purpose."[9]

William Temple, archbishop of Canterbury in mid-twentieth century, said that the church was the only society in the world that

7. Frazier, "Church as Sign," 5–6.
8. Ibid., 13.
9. Ibid.

existed for its nonmembers. His statement urged the church to embrace an outward (not inward) focus, to be a sign of the reign.

An ecumenical consensus developed in the 1970s and 1980s that gave support for this missional understanding of the church for Roman Catholics, Protestants and Orthodox Christians. More and more, across the spectrum of Christianity a common phraseology emerged that talked of the church as a sign, a preview and an instrument of the reign of God.

Jesus proclaimed the coming of the reign of God (Mark 1:15; Matt 4:23). He beckoned followers to form a community of disciples in service to the Good News of the coming reign. The church is not to be equated with the reign of God. The church is a community that points to it (*sign*), a community that anticipates it (*preview*), a community that is an active agent in bringing about the justice and mercy that God intends for all creation (*instrument*).

What greater sign is there for our world today than a group of persons of diverse ethnic and racial backgrounds breaking bread together in the name of Jesus! On laity Sunday, Rebeca Trujillo preached at the New Brunswick United Methodist Church in New Brunswick, New Jersey. Rebeca chose the Twenty-Third Psalm as the Scripture lesson on which to preach. When she began, she looked across the congregation and saw people of more than thirty nations and as many colors as in Noah's rainbow. In this English-speaking worship service, she invited hearers to remember the opening lines of this most familiar psalm. "When I was a child," said Rebeca, "I learned the words, 'El Señor es mi pastor, nada me faltará.' What other languages can we use to say these same words?"

"The Lord is my shepherd, I shall not want," said Bernice. "I learned that in Nebraska, where I grew up."

Others began chiming in, reciting the famous line in Chinese, Tagalog, Urdu, Greek, French, Shona, and Twi. There were many languages, but one verse from the Bible was held in common. After several more people shared, others in the congregation stood and began to applaud in what became an explosion of celebratory affirmation that though they were many, they were one.

As a *sign*, the church points to something greater than itself. It points to God's realm where the love of God and the God of love permeate every aspect of life. The church is "sign" when it comes together for worship. In worship, the church lifts up songs of praise to the ruler of the universe. The church confesses that its own behavior falls short of the design of the Creator. The church confesses the sin of not living according to the spirit and rule of God's reign.

Too often churches point inwardly, to themselves. Members of the congregation view worship as a form of entertainment. If the music isn't to their liking or the sermon takes an unpopular position, they become critics. They expect worship to meet their own needs.

When a church is a sign, the attitude of parishioners changes completely. Rather than seeking to have their own needs met, congregants lose themselves in the act of worship. Their focus is on God and giving honor and glory to God through liturgy, song, praise, prayer, preaching. When people outside the congregation observe this kind of worship, they exclaim, "Look how they adore their God!" By losing themselves in the worship experience, they find themselves (cf. Mark 8:35).

The church is not a sign for itself, but rather a sign for others. The church does not "perform" for the sake of others, but rather is characterized by such adoration for God, such love for Jesus Christ that its witness wins people without prodding them.

God allows us a *preview* of God's reign in the life of the church. It often comes in the moment when a baby is baptized or the cup of communion is shared. We rehearse what it will be like to live in God's reign, when the love of God overflows the community of believers, when God's Spirit and presence penetrate our hearts. This *koinonia*, this intimate communion of the Holy Spirit, one with another, has been described by Protestants, Roman Catholics, and Orthodox Christians as a "preview" of the coming reign of God.[10] Henri Nouwen called it a breakthrough when Christian

---

10. See *The Nature and Mission of the Church: A Stage on the Way to a Common Statement*, Faith and Order Paper 198, December 2005, available from the World Council of Churches website: http://www.oikoumene.org/

community so shines a light for humanity that those who watch can only exclaim, "See how they love each other!"[11]

While my sister Bev is cooking her famous homemade vegetable soup, I invariably ask for a taste while it is still simmering. My usual response to her upon the sampling is, "Oh what a foretaste of glory divine!" Just by that foretaste I know the soup will be good that day.

The church, when it lives out its calling, is a foretaste or preview of the divine community of love in God's reign. When the members of the community of faith live out Jesus' command to love one another (John 13:34), they anticipate God's universal commonwealth of love.

The New Testament word for the loving communion of the fellowship of believers is *koinonia*. It refers to the fellowship of sharing the love of Christ in community. Believers also share the Holy Spirit and they are linked to one another in service and faith. In the first letter of John, the term *koinonia* refers to the living bond that unites followers of Jesus (1 John 1:3).

Through the love, fellowship, and communion of the community of believers, the church anticipates what it is like to live within the rule of God. It becomes a preview of the glory divine. The unconditional love experienced within community is patterned on the love of God for God's people. This love shared in fellowship contrasts with the way people relate to one another in secular society.

The church is a preview in that through the love we have for one another we experience what it will be like to live in God's reign. It is as if in the church we are constantly rehearsing what it will be like to live in God's reign by the way we love and care for one another, the way we serve others, and the way we worship God.

---

en/resources/documents/commissions/faith-and-order/i-unity-the-church-and-its-mission/the-nature-and-mission-of-the-church-a-stage-on-the-way-to-a-common-statement. The Roman Catholic Church uses the language of "sacrament" for *preview*, referring to sacrament in a general sense. See "*Lumen Gentium* (Dogmatic Constitution on the Church)," in *Documents of Vatican II*, 15.

11. Nouwen, *Clowning in Rome*, 8–9.

A Peter Scholtes song carries the refrain, "They'll know we are Christians by our love."[12] When others see the love shared within a Christian community, when the love is palpable even to those outside the community of faith, that Christian community is a preview of living in God's reign.

Can we live and love within our churches in such a way that others, observing us, will exclaim, "Look how they love one another!"? Does the church practice forgiveness and reconciliation (cf. Matt 6:14)? Is it focused on God's reign above all other things (cf. Matt 6:33)?

Jesus came that we may have life and have it abundantly (John 10:10). He wanted all humanity to know the wonder and fullness of life. The church, as God's called community, works as an instrument of God's reign so that people in the world might know and experience the promise of life.

The church does not wait for the consummation of God's victory that brings God's justice and love into the world. The church acts as an *instrument* of God's reign to relieve suffering, advocate for justice, and minister to its immediate community and beyond in the too-real situations of human life.

The church understands the immediate context in which it ministers, and as it proclaims and embodies the gospel of life, it affirms the dignity of humanity, defends human life, restores and celebrates humankind. As an instrument of the reign of God, the people who come together to form Christian community strive to be people who see and do things differently.

They strive to serve, not dominate; forgive, not judge; seek reconciliation, not revenge. They strive to feed the hungry and visit those in prison without drawing attention to themselves or expect anything in return. They recognize injustice and advocate fairness. As Stephen E. Fowl and L. Gregory Jones have written, "They are more concerned about others' welfare than their own, the kind of people willing to risk their lives so that others may live."[13]

12. Scholtes, "They'll Know We Are Christians by Our Love," in United Methodist Church, *The Faith We Sing*, no. 2223.

13. Fowl and Jones, *Reading in Communion*, 78.

New Canaan United Methodist Church in Kearny, New Jersey, is located in a lower-income suburb of New York City. There are large immigrant communities that attend New Canaan, principally from Portuguese-language countries like Brazil, Portugal, Angola and Mozambique. Problems endemic to this community include crime, prostitution, and violence. New Canaan has offered workshops to immigrants on how to navigate the US credit card system and how to be a good steward of funds. It has provided a deep sense of community, *koinonia,* for persons who have traveled far from their country of origin. It has met people at their point of need. Today the church includes former "Go-Go Girls" who have left potential riches behind to embrace a healthy and wholesome life as Christians. New Canaan knew that to be effective in its community, it needed to serve as an *instrument* of God's reign. In the process of reaching out to the needs of the immediate area, New Canaan helped transform the lives of many people.

Inagrace Dietterich is the Director of Theological Research for the Center for Parish Development in Chicago, Illinois. Dr. Dietterich could well have been describing New Canaan Church when she helped define this framework for the mission of the church: "The church is called not only to be a holy people at worship, or a community of mutual love and service, but also an apostolic instrument of God's mission. . . . As the body of Christ in the world, the church is God's primary agent of healing, forgiveness, and transformation."[14]

The church is called by God to be a sign, preview, and instrument of God's reign. As congregations engage the road to renewal, they are invited to rediscover their mission within this larger framework, affirmed by an ecumenical consensus of Christian churches. In addition to denominational scorecards that tend to measure numbers, today's churches can measure themselves as a sign, preview and instrument of the reign of God. As more congregations begin to point the way, to anticipate, and to serve as agents of what some call "the beloved community," we will all come just a bit nearer to that blessed destination.

14. Dietterich and McCoy, "Sign, Foretaste, and Instrument," 13.

The church, in its rediscovery of the real-life situations of the people it is called to serve, responds to the need to educate children and begins a school. It sees the need to provide medical care and organizes a health clinic. It witnesses neglect of the elderly in its community and advocates for senior citizen services. The church serves as an instrument of God's reign for all people living in the community. The church may have to play an unpopular role in society by denouncing injustice and personal or corporate sin. It may be called to risk its life to be an instrument of God's reign.

The church is an "instrument" of God's reign when it works for the values of the reign: helping to alleviate human suffering, reaching out to meet the needs of the community and the world in which we live. Many of our churches do a good job as "instruments." Historically, the people called Methodist have engaged in ministries of mercy, reaching out to those in prison, those who are sick, and those who are left behind in society. When such service is truly altruistic, it becomes part of an overall spirit that pervades the community of faith. Those outside the community exclaim, "Look how they love and serve their fellow human beings!" The mission-oriented church rediscovers the needs of its surrounding community and world and carries out ministry to address those needs.

As it embarks on the road to renewal, the leadership team navigating the journey decides how it will measure success. What will our scorecard look like? It can add to denominational requirements what we might call a "Reign of God values" scorecard that measures the mission and ministry of the church in terms of being a sign, preview, and instrument of the reign of God. The "reality check" assesses the starting point of the church and begins to gain clarity on what a preferred future would look like.

Your Turn

1. What does it mean to say that the reign of God is a commonwealth of love or blessed community of love or God's

new society? How do these terms confirm or challenge your understanding of the reign of God?

2. Would you characterize your church as more "sanctuary" oriented or "sign" oriented?

3. In what ways would those outside the fellowship of your church view your church as a *sign* of the reign of God?

4. In what ways would those outside of the fellowship of your church view your church as a *preview* of the reign of God?

5. In what ways would those outside of the fellowship of your church view your church as an *instrument* of the reign of God?

6. What is keeping your church from being more fully a sign, preview and instrument of the reign of God? What needs to change in the life of your church to reflect better being sign, preview and instrument of the reign of God?

7. What are the items that your "scorecard" uses to measure church effectiveness?

2

Reconnect

IT IS GOOD TO pray before embarking on *any* trip regardless of its length or purpose. The *Washington Post* has reported grim statistics about the danger of driving. Globally, more than 1.2 million people die each year in traffic accidents. Another fifty million people are injured. "Road deaths are now the number-one global killer of people aged 10 to 24. . . . More people die as a result of traffic accidents than are killed by major scourges such as malaria or diabetes."[1]

When I start on a long road trip, I begin with a word of prayer. Praying for travel mercies makes sense. When we are driving, our journey can be affected by weather conditions, careless driving on the part of others, and distractions. We are wise to center ourselves in God before starting. Occasionally, my bishop asked that I pick him up when we were to go to the same meeting. The time in the car afforded us a chance to talk. Before I put the car in gear to depart, he always asked that we pray. Prayer before a road trip always make sense regardless of the distance to drive.

Similarly, we want to direct our attention to God as we begin the journey for church renewal—hopefully a journey that takes us to where God wants our church to be. We know that the journey can be dangerous. We may encounter conflict on the way as those from among our fellowship share differing visions of where we

1. Mundell, "U.N. Seeks to Curb World's Traffic Deaths."

ought to go. If we embark on plans that require change, some will resist. It is important to involve the entire congregation in prayer as church leadership navigates the road to renewal. How comforting for those on the road to know that folks back home are praying for them!

Prayer is at the heart of the roadway to renewal. As a church begins on this journey together, *prayer* needs to be at the center of all that it does. We need prayer warriors, prayer teams and corporate prayer.

As we take to the road for renewal, picture a van large enough for the leadership team, which could be from six to fifteen passengers. This team will travel the road on behalf of the entire community of faith. It will report on the progress it makes and stay in communication with the folks back home.

Prayer Warriors

As a young pastor I was appointed to a two-point charge in an urban area. Average attendance was fifty at the first church and thirty at the second. When I arrived for my first Sunday—a good half hour before the first church's service was to begin—I was greeted by Edward, a burly, middle-aged man. Edward was a prayer warrior.

"Pastor, we have a prayer meeting before each service," said Edward. "We would welcome your participation, but please know that it is completely up to you. I know some pastors like to go over their sermon just before a service."

"I would like to join you," I said.

"We would be delighted," he said and then added, "We will hold our prayer meeting whether or not you can join us—we just wanted to make sure you knew you were invited."

About fifteen minutes prior to worship, Edward and about six others would join hands and pray. They would pray for the people who would be filling the pews that day and praying that every pew space be filled. They prayed for families they knew would not be able to attend due to illness or travel. They would pray that the Holy Spirit inspire the hearts and souls of all those who worshipped with us that morning.

I could not help but notice the difference in vitality of the first church of this two-point charge from the second point. While the liturgy was the same, there was more passion at the first service. The prayer warriors, led by Edward, made all the difference. The road to renewal needs the help of prayer warriors like Edward to pray traveling mercies for every step, every mile of the way. We also need prayer warriors to go in the van with us. The entire journey needs to be infused with prayer.

Listen to God / Listen to One Another

Just as it is important to pray before starting off on the journey, it is equally important to listen to God throughout the journey. Prayer is the art of calling out and listening to God. Psalm 34, one of the psalms attributed to David, reminds us of this:

> I sought the Lord, and he answered me,
> and delivered me from all my fears.
> Look to him, and be radiant;
> so your faces shall never be ashamed.
> This poor soul cried, and was heard by the Lord,
> and was saved from every trouble.
> The angel of the Lord encamps
> around those who fear him, and delivers them.
> O taste and see that the Lord is good;
> happy are those who take refuge in him. (Ps 34:4–8)

God speaks to us through the Scriptures. God speaks to us through the meditative word spoken in sermons. God speaks to us in the interchange of ideas that comes when we practice personal and group devotions. In your journey toward renewal, those who travel together take turns leading the group in reflecting on Scripture readings. Together we seek God. We seek deliverance from fears of the future, fears of what may be encountered on the road. We seek God to deliver us from troubles. The happiness of which David speaks comes when we take refuge in God, seeking him earnestly.

During the summers between college years I served as a counselor at a church camp. The children came for a week of outdoors fun that included hiking, swimming, sports and games along with "morning watch" when we would find a quiet place in the woods to read the Bible and pray as well as group singing around the campfire. One of the highlights of the week was our excursion to Sunrise Mountain. We would load up a van with campers and travel about fifteen miles to a mountaintop gazebo located along the Appalachian Trail. While the mountain was called "Sunrise," we went to see the sun set. We would take off after dinner arriving in time for a worship service in the gazebo. We read Scripture, sang songs and invariably there was a sense of wonder as we saw the sun dip down beyond the next mountain range. We would cheer for God's creation.

Often the real fun was in the van going or coming from the mountain. We would break out in song as the children rocked the van with raucous delight. This indescribable joy penetrated the deepest part of the soul. God spoke to us through community, through the laughter and joy of being together. God spoke to us in the journey. More than half the fun was in getting to Sunrise Mountain.

More than half the fun of the road to renewal are the discoveries we experience as community when we are on the way. God speaks to us in unscripted moments. We seek God as we journey and God finds us as we make discoveries about ourselves and about our church. God speaks to us in the moments of enlightenment when something that had been heretofore unknown or confusing suddenly becomes meaningfully illuminated.

To be aware of these illuminations, we need to *listen* and listen carefully. How and where is God speaking to us as we journey toward renewal? Is God giving us signs along the road that are important to notice? Has someone in the group stumbled upon an insight that can spark our imaginations as to where God wants to lead us? Lest we miss these epiphanies, we need to cultivate a culture of listening to one another and God. Dietrich Bonhoeffer, the martyred German theologian and head of an alternative seminary during the time when Hitler was chancellor, said that "the *first* service one owes to another in community is listening to him."[2]

Perhaps there is nothing more frustrating than trying to explain something to someone who is not listening. Listening incorporates much more that the physical act of hearing. Hearing depends on the physical capacity of our ears. Listening is done with an inner ear of understanding. The listener gives thoughtful consideration to what is being said in order to understand what the speaker is saying. When a person listens, she opens herself to dialogue.

Listening creates a free and sacred space of acceptance and love. Morton T. Kelsey, an Episcopal priest who taught at the University of Notre Dame, and the author of more than twenty books, including *Companions on the Inner Way*, holds that true listening is a form of loving. He writes, "We simply can't pretend to love anyone to whom we do not listen. Listening gives the first sign to a person that he or she has worth and is valuable enough to be attended to."[3]

Clarifying Your Witness

One of the shortcomings of mainline Protestantism in the twenty-first-century United States is the reluctance to tell each other our faith stories. At least, that has been my experience in churches in the Northeast. As a church embarks on the road to renewal, one important exercise is for leaders to get in touch with their personal witness for Jesus Christ.

One of the reasons, perhaps, that churchgoers are reluctant to give witness to their faith is that they don't want to be associated

2. Bonhoeffer, *Life Together*, 98.
3. Kelsey, *Companions on the Inner Way*, 202.

with the aggressive proselytizers who come on so strong that they turn people away.

On April 30, 2008, the General Conference of the United Methodist Church voted to add "to be faithful in their witness" to the list of vows one takes upon becoming a member of the church. From that time on, those joining a United Methodist Church promise to be faithful through their prayers, presence, gifts, service *and witness*.[4]

Adding "witness" to the familiar litany of vows a member accepts and practices, underscores its importance. Perhaps today, more than ever, we need to make our witness to faith in Jesus Christ much more evident. The inclusion of witness in the membership vows gives impetus to this. Leaders traveling the road to renewal would be wise to remember their vow to witness.

What does it mean to "witness"? The dictionary defines "witness" as having personal knowledge of something and giving testimony to it. One is an observer of an event and then is able to tell others what one has seen or heard. As Christians, we can witness to the knowledge we have of Jesus Christ and the meaning he has for our lives. Our response to simple questions such as "Do you go to church?" or "Are you a Christian?" is an opening to witness to our faith. After that opening we can share with another person what we know about faith, our faith.

Giving witness, though, is even more than sharing what we know. The first Christian historian, Eusebius, defined witness as the way one lived. He called it *philosophou biou*—a philosophy of life or, more accurately, our way of life. We give witness by the way we live. John Wesley emphasized this through what is now known as "Wesley's Rule": "Do all the good you can, by all the means you can, in all the ways you can, in all the places you can, at all the times you can, to all the people you can, as long as you ever can." It is to live out the promise of the familiar song refrain: "They will know we are Christians by our love."

I was privileged to be part of one of the first Volunteer in Mission Team trips to Cuba. A dozen of us from New York and

4. *Book of Discipline of the United Methodist Church*, para. 217.6.

New Jersey went to a small town called San Juan de las Yeras in the central part of the island. At the time, early 1990s, a visiting group from the United States was a rarity. Children stayed home from school just to look at us. We formed brigades to complete needed projects. One team painted the inside walls of the church. I was on the team that replaced the tin roof. There had been so many holes in the roof that sunlight streamed in to the sanctuary like white laser lights.

Because of my fluency in Spanish I served as translator for the roof team between the volunteers who had come from the United States and the Cuban hired workers from the town. The Cuban workers were not members of the church but rather specialists in this kind of work. In fact, they declared that they were not Christian at all.

The tin roof panels were purchased from the only Cuban factory that made them. Many of them were not square, which made it nearly impossible to line them up correctly as we laid them on the studs. Our team leader, Roy, with the help of the Cubans hired for the week, tried to make the tin panels fit. In the Cuba of that day, there was little to no competition. We bought the tin panels from the only supplier available—the government. It was frustrating to try to match panels that were not cut straight.

Roy showed an extra measure of grace and patience that week. He discussed with the Cuban workers how to overcome the shortcomings of the materials. His normal demeanor of quiet confidence and kindness began to leave an impact on the hired Cubans. They would communicate with each other through my translation. I couldn't help but notice how the workers gained a greater amount of respect for Roy as the week wore on and they struggled to complete the job of roofing with inadequate materials. The day before we were to leave, as we were making the final tin panels fit onto the roof, one of the Cuban workers looked at me and pointed to Roy. "If that is what it means to be a Christian," he said, "sign me up!"

Later that day he gave his life to Christ asking Roy to pray for him. Through everyday interaction Roy gave witness to his faith.

He didn't have to preach a sermon. There were no formulaic invitations to salvation. His lifestyle was the witness, the *philosophou biou*.

A third understanding of witness, in addition to sharing what we know and the example of our lifestyle, goes to the root of the word—literally. The Greek word that we translate for witness is *martys* from which we also receive the English word, martyr. To give witness is to be willing to give our all for the Cause to which we testify. It is to take risks for the knowledge we have of Jesus Christ. Such witness brings others to the faith. It was Tertullian who wrote that "the blood of the martyrs is seed." When something is worth dying for, others want to know what it is.

As you journey on the road to renewal, gather the members of the leadership team to spend time helping one another to articulate their witness. As we prepare for the trip ahead, spend time sharing faith stories with one another. The idea is to gain clarity of what our personal testimony is. How do we answer questions such as, "What does Jesus Christ mean to you?" or "Why do you believe in Jesus Christ?" or "Why do you belong to the church?" To give witness, we need to be prepared to answer these kinds of questions. We might write what our answers are on a sheet of paper, or compose a lyric to a song, or paint a picture that expresses what Christ means to us.

Before setting out on the road, share with each other faith stories. In addition to providing a forum for gaining clarity about our personal witness, sharing of deep beliefs will help the leadership team know one another better. It will serve to build team spirit and trust.

Team Building

If we want our church to serve as a "preview" of the reign of God, we need to instill the sense of *koinonia* that fuels such community spirit. The presence of *koinonia* should be replicated in the small groups of the church. Nowhere is this more important than in the leadership team that navigates the road to renewal. We need to

come to the realization that we are in the same van together jour-
neying toward the better, more preferred future that God has in
store for our church.

The manager of a professional baseball team asks his players
to check their egos at the door. He wants them to suppress their
desire to enhance individual statistics for the sake of winning as
a team. This is the value of humility, where the leader and team
member keep ego, pride and self-importance in check for the sake
of the larger issue, namely, the transformation of individual lives
and communities because of a relationship with Jesus Christ and
the reign he inaugurated.

The team that maintains openness, listens to new ideas and
suggestions, however bizarre, is one that exercises leadership. It is
vital that the leadership team find ways to open channels of communication with the congregation at large. Ownership on the part
of the entire congregation for plans and decisions needs to be built.
The value of openness and the willingness to listen and value every
member of the organization will lead the congregation success-
fully on the road to renewal.

Ground Rules

A good practice for the leadership team taking the road to renewal
is setting ground rules for the way they will behave with each
other. When we begin to talk about the future of the church and
possible routes to take, passion rises. People get excited. This is a
good thing. We want to encourage people to engage the road pas-
sionately. However, sometimes in the midst of the excitement we
can forget who we are as Christians and behave in a way that does
dishonor to our calling. Set ground rules from the get-go. Ask the
group how they want to behave with one another.

Wesley's rules can help immensely at this point. Rueben P.
Job's *Three Simple Rules* distills John Wesley's General Rules (given
to newly formed Methodist societies in 1739 England) into three
memorable rules for life: (1) Do no harm, (2) do good, and (3) stay
in love with God.

These rules apply to any Christian of any church or denomination. They can serve as "the rule of life" for intentional community. I will not rehearse the entire book here. For our purposes on the road to renewal, the three rules provide concise ground rules to mark our behavior with one another as we navigate the journey together. I encourage the reader to purchase a copy of Rueben Job's book and keep it always close by. It is a resource for life.

Come up with your own ground rules as well. How will you make sure you listen to one another and respect each person's input? One group established the ground rule of not allowing others to finish their sentences and refraining from the temptation to speak for another or to finish their thoughts. Another group laid down ground rules for attendance at meetings and completion of assignments between meetings. When these guidelines are discussed and agreed upon at the outset of the journey, it can help smooth over tense moments later on. Post the ground rules on newsprint in your meeting room so they are a constant reminder and a ready reference if someone strays from them.

Wesley's simple rule of "staying in love with God" is especially important in the context of keeping the journey in prayer at all times. Form prayer partners at the beginning of the journey. Covenant to pray with one other member of the team. This can be done in a variety of ways: by agreeing to engage in daily prayer at the same time of the day; by calling one another daily to pray together; by exchanging prayer blogs, texts or emails. If we are to reconnect with the mission that God has envisioned for our church, prayer must be the center of our discernment as we journey the road to renewal. Spend time at each meeting of the entire group to share experiences of your prayer partnership.

Invite the congregation to join you in prayer. Ask the congregation to keep the leadership team in prayer. You may want to include "mission moments" during worship when people can give witness to their prayer partnerships. If your church has a "prayer chain" make sure that the work of the leadership team is included on the list of people and situations to pray for.

Your Turn

Prayer

Form prayer partnerships from among the members of the leadership team. A prayer partnership includes two or three persons. During the weeks ahead, be attentive to the prayer concerns lifted up in worship. Draw upon the information gathered as you work your way through the *Roadmap to Renewal* to formulate a prayer plan where the pressing concerns raised and the people most affected by these concerns are kept before your partnership. Prayer partners are invited to pray for these concerns prior to gathering at regularly scheduled worship. Individuals in the prayer partnership are asked to pray for the concerns and people during daily devotional time.

1. What can you do together as a leadership team to assure that your road to renewal is undergirded always with prayer?

2. How can you involve the congregation in upholding the road to renewal in prayer?

Faith Stories

Gather together as a leadership team to share faith stories. Come to the meeting prepared to share a one-page account of what Jesus Christ means to you and what church membership means to you. After reading this chapter, respond to the following questions together.

1. What do your faith stories share in common?

2. What is different about the stories shared?

3. What lessons can we draw from hearing one another's faith journey that will help us understand how people enter a relationship with Christ in our church and community?

Teamwork

1. Describe a time when you felt a part of a team.

2. What made it a team (i.e., what were the team's characteristics)?

3. Why is it important that the leadership team work as a team?

4. What are the ground rules that could help us achieve teamwork?

3

Rediscover the Landscape of Our Parish

WHEN THE APOSTLE PAUL started on missionary journeys, he learned to adapt the way in which he presented the gospel according to the culture and characteristics of the people. The gospel he preached to Jews was nuanced to appeal to the needs of Jews. The gospel presented to Greeks was presented in a way they could hear and understand.

In his first letter to the Corinthians Paul described his approach: "To the Jews I became a Jew, in order to win Jews. To those under the law I became as one under the law (though I myself am not under the law) so that I might win those under the law. . . . I have become all things to all people, that I might by all means save some. I do it all for the sake of the gospel, so that I may share in its blessings" (1 Cor 9:20–23).

Paul knew that he needed to understand the people to whom he was preaching and teaching in order to present the gospel in a way that could be heard and understood. Paul took care to understand the demographics of the people he engaged. "Demographics" refer to the characteristics of populations. The root words, "demo" and "graphic" refer to the statistics of people. Paul wanted to know the characteristics of people and was aware of how he himself needed to adapt "for the sake of the gospel, so that I may share in its blessings" (1 Cor 9:23).

Traveling the road to renewal includes taking a fresh look at the demographics of the community in which your church is located. You can do this through analysis of data, driving around the area your church serves, and by holding informal and formal conversations with people who live in your town or city.

Mission Insite (http://missioninsite.com) offers excellent demographic data for congregations. Most mainline denominations have accounts with Mission Insite that enable laity or clergy to access essential information to get to know their parish area better. Every annual conference of The United Methodist Church in the USA is a client of Mission Insite. Check with your denomination to see if your church association or judicatory has access to this service.

Think of data as a core asset of your church. When you dig deeper to understand the people who live in your parish area, you will gain greater knowledge of them and acquire the ability to make authentic connections. The key ingredient for the best use of Mission Insite involves plotting your people on the maps they provide. Follow the instructions on the website to upload the addresses of members and friends of the church. Zoom into geographical clusters so that you can answer the following questions about the people you seek to serve: Who are we? Who are our neighbors? What missional connections can we make with the people living in our area? Mission Insite offers information on three essential views of people living in your area: a core view that will help you understand who they are and their cultural proclivities; a community view that describes the mission field in which you are placed; and a fusion view that will offer ways that can shape your ministry so that you can more fully engage the population you are serving. The data will give you information about race, ethnicity, economics, percentage of school-age children and much more.

The Mission Insite web presence offers easy-to-use menus to help you engage your population area. Learn about the segments of the population that are living in your midst. Read about the mosaic groupings and then hold conversations in your church and with focus groups in the community to develop missional strategies that will address needs and yearnings of people.

You will want to track the demographic changes that occur in your parish area. Find out who is moving in. What are their age groupings? What racial and ethnic backgrounds are represented? You will want to compare the community data of demographics with your own internal demographics of the church. The key question is: "Does our church reflect the community in which we are located?"

If you find differences between how the town looks and how your church looks, begin to ask why. Often I have heard churches that give facile answers for apparent gaps. They claim that one religion predominates or a new immigrant group moving in would not be interested in attending their church. Resist the temptation to find easy answers for more complex information.

Hackensack, New Jersey, experienced an influx of immigrants from the Caribbean in the 1970s and 1980s. Many had been members of the Methodist Church of the Caribbean and the Americas in their homeland. Upon arriving in Hackensack they visited the local United Methodist Church. At first members of the largely Anglo congregation did not know how to welcome these newcomers. They missed opportunities to welcome people who had been lifelong Methodists. Eventually, when the church became more aware of demographic changes, they learned how much they shared in a common religious heritage. Many of their new neighbors joined the church.

The worldwide reach of the church means that some folk who come from foreign lands may have been reared in churches that were the result of missionary activity of churches in the United States. They have a natural proclivity to seek out a church that is familiar. They need to find a church home that reminds them of their land of origin. Demographic research along with an awareness of the historical mission of the church can help uncover new neighbors to reach. Learn of the possible connections by contacting your denominational mission leadership and by visiting their websites.

Driving Around

Here is a chance to make the analogy of driving the road to renewal a literal experience! Take the leadership team on a drive through the area served by your church. You may consider your church's region as covering several towns or even a county. Assign someone to take notes as you drive through different parts of your area and discuss what you see. "Why is that factory closed?" "Why is that home boarded up?" "How many homes will be built in that new housing development? What will they cost?"

Heretofore downtrodden cities along the Hudson River of New Jersey have gone through a metamorphous during the past thirty years. Areas that included warehouses, tenements and abandoned factories have been undergoing a change that has brought luxury condominiums, loft residences, high-end retailers and improved public transportation. The gentrification of these areas has forced residents to sell their homes and move away for they no longer can afford the higher taxes. Some of our churches in these areas have experienced a loss of membership because of these changes.

The challenge to our existing churches is whether or not they can change with the times. Can they minister to these new residents? With whom can they partner to engage in new ministries? These kinds of changes become obvious when we take time to drive around and see them, and asking questions.

Compile the questions raised by driving around and begin to find answers. Some answers can be found through research: reviewing newspaper articles online or in the library; obtaining copies of the city, town or county's master plan for development. Other answers will come by talking to people in the neighborhoods where these changes are occurring.

Ministry by Walking Around

Formulate a list of questions raised as a result of driving around that you can ask people in the neighborhoods. Test demographic research by asking questions of real people. The information gained from demographic research always needs to be paired with information gathered from meeting people in the neighborhood. It is important to get out of the car!

At a School of Congregational Development years ago, I participated in a case study for starting a new church in the Allston area of Boston. The demographic information in the notebook we were handed indicated that a high percentage of the population were single young adults. There were many colleges and graduate schools in the vicinity of the area studied. As we worked together as a team we began to brainstorm how a church could be planted among a population of single young adults. Then, we took a public transit line to the Allston area. We split into teams of two and began canvassing the area asking simple questions like, "What is the greatest need of this neighborhood?"

We were surprised when we came back together that so many people indicated that the needs of children were paramount. Over and over we heard from people in diners and passersby on the street that "there is nothing for kids to do in this area." Had we missed something in our demographic analysis?

We went back to the demographic notebook and discovered that young married couples with children were the second highest population profile in the area. We had to rethink completely what it would mean to plant a new church in Allston. We learned an important lesson. Demographic information must always be tested by talking with real people in actual neighborhoods.

This experience gave rise to what I came to call "Ministry by Walking Around," or MBWA for short. In the feedback received from users of *The Discovery Church Journey*, many found helpful the sessions that got them out of their churches talking to people in neighborhoods. It is important to note that this kind of exercise is done for the purpose of gathering data. You are not trying to get people to come to church or preach the gospel. Not yet. The idea is to gather information so that your church can make connections with the community in which it is placed.

"Ministry by Walking Around" can also help answer questions raised by driving around. In teams of two or three, walk around the neighborhood and town center. In rural areas this may be the local convenience store, truck stop, or post office where people gather. Talk to people about their perceptions of your church and their perceptions of the needs of the community. Talk to real estate agents, law enforcement officers, social workers, school personnel, merchants, and people on the street or in stores. Identify yourselves as members of a local area church and ask people if they are willing to respond to several questions. Questions to ask include:

1. How long have you lived in this community?

2. Where does one go for spiritual help in this community?

3. Is there anything about (insert your church name) that makes a difference for the people of this community? What is it known for?

4. What are the most pressing needs of this community?

5. What are the deepest spiritual yearnings of this community? Are they being met? By whom?

6. What assets already exist in the community (skills, library)? And how can we in the church help pull these assets together for the benefit of the community?

Add your own questions to this list, which are mere suggestions, to get you started. After canvassing the area, meet with other pairs to share findings. Ask questions like these:

1. What did we learn about our community through the conversations we held with people this afternoon?

2. What were some of the needs of the community that were articulated?

3. How well is our church serving as an instrument to meet those needs?

4. What were some of the assets or resources that the community has?

5. Where are people going for spiritual help and what are some of their spiritual and emotional needs?

6. How do people see our church? What do they know about us and think of us?

The Pitman UMC in Pitman, New Jersey, engaged in a MBWA exercise as they sought to find their road to the future. Their 1895 church building was destroyed by fire. Built before the age of the automobile, they had to decide whether to rebuild on the same plot of land or relocate to new property where they could include a parking lot. It wasn't a simple question. The town had been built around the church. It was named for the first pastor of the church. Even though the church had no parking, for many it was the center of town and the town's identity.

They asked people in the neighborhood about their perception of the church. "You know that church that burned down?" they would ask people on the street. "What is it known for?" People responded by saying things like, "Oh, that church has a great history" or "The town was founded around that church" or "It was a great landmark."

The members of Pitman asking the questions realized that the church was known for its history but not its current ministry. Engaging in MBWA was an important part of listening to the community to gain a new perspective of who they were. The church members wanted to be known for their present day ministry and not as a historical icon.

When it came time to decide whether to rebuild on the old plot of land or relocate, Pitman UMC decided to relocate. They concluded that they needed to build a facility for ministry in the twenty-first century and not a monument to the past. The information gathered in Ministry by Walking Around helped clarify the way forward.

Talking to Town Leaders

Talking to town leaders is another exercise that gets folk out of the church and into the community. It involves talking with elected officials, influential citizens, and businesspeople to gain a new perspective on the community. Whereas MBWA is a more informal way of gathering information, talking to town leaders is formal. We encourage teams of two to make arrangements to interview people. Try to talk with the mayor or town council member; officers of the parent teacher organization; officers of service clubs like the Kiwanis or Rotary; representatives of the police and fire departments; and school officials. Also talk with the influential leaders of town who are recognized because of the long time their business has been in the community. A good place to visit is the popular barber shop or beauty salon.

Plan to take no more than twenty minutes of their time. Always make an appointment. Clearly state the purpose of the interview—to gather information about the community so that the church can make connections with its needs. Identify yourself and your church. Ask for permission to take notes. Offer the person interviewed to review your notes when finished. Thank the interviewee for her time and information. Offer to send a summary of the church's findings.

Another way to accomplish this is by hosting a "leader's forum luncheon" where the persons you might interview individually are brought together in one place. Ask the town leaders to share their perspectives on the community.

Formulate a list of interview questions. Use variations of the following questions as a starting point: (1) What do we see as the major issues the community has to face? (2) What steps are being taken to deal with these issues? (3) What should the community do about these issues? (4) Are there ways the church can help? (5) What assets and opportunities exist and are perhaps overlooked that help define this community and its potential?

Include additional questions that arose as you were driving around the area. Go beyond the answers you may have found through researching newspapers and ask town council members why the factory closed or what is happening to displaced residents as a result of gentrification. Try to work with the people so that possible partnerships can be forged.

A church in Basin, Wyoming, made arrangements to talk with executives of the local soft drink bottling plant about the needs of the community. The executives wanted to know why the church was seeking this information. When they explained that they were trying to discover the needs of the community and how they might meet those needs, the executives became interested. Eventually the church and the bottling plant forged a partnership to address issues of hunger and homelessness in the area. It never would have happened if the church hadn't initiated the conversation. There is no telling how rich the movement of the spirit will be when churches and people in the community begin to dialogue about needs in the area.

Your Turn

Obtain demographic information about the area that your church serves. Contact a denominational representative to learn how to access Mission Insite. Organize a time and day when the leadership team can drive around the area served by your church. Make notes of your observations and questions. Set aside a time when the leadership team can go out in twos or threes to engage in Ministry by Walking Around (MBWA). Formulate a list of questions to ask people.

Assign team members to make appointments with town leaders for formal interviews. Gather the information as outlined in this chapter and bring it back to the larger group.

1. What did you learn about your community by "Driving Around?"

2. What did you learn via the conversations held through "Ministry by Walking Around?"

3. What did the community teach you about your church? Does perception match reality? Why or why not?

4. From the data gathered both informally and formally, what are the pressing needs of the community in which the church is located?

4

Reassess Our Current Ministry

WE HAVE DRIVEN AROUND the area that our church serves. We have studied the lay of the land using demographics. We have stopped at various spots in the area to talk with people in formal and informal ways. We are gaining clarity of discerning where God wants us to go. That is, we know that we want to end up in a place much better than where we currently are. We want to discover along the road new insights that will make our community of faith stronger, more self-sufficient, and better connected to the larger community to which we belong. And we want that end-up-place to align with God's design for our particular community of faith.

Every road trip needs a driver and a navigator. Sometimes we take turns driving. The driver calls people to get on board but once we get going, he keeps both eyes on the road. The navigator keeps the vehicle on track. He or she moderates the discussion of those in the vehicle (those at a leadership team meeting). A "Guided Process Servant" or coach comes alongside the navigator to help keep the vehicle moving forward.

As we set out on the road to rediscover the church's mission, the navigator turns to the people on board, the leadership team, and asks some pointed questions. The questions are designed to help all of us gain further clarity about our identity as a church.

What Can We Celebrate about Our Church's Journey Up to Now?

Sometimes the decision to take the road to renewal brings resistance. "What is wrong with the way things are now?" people may ask. "Why do we need to take this journey?" These are important questions. You don't want to deny the wonderful and positive attributes of the church. As you embark on the journey, you will want to assess what is truly valuable about who you have been and what you have been doing as a church.

Start by asking what we can celebrate about our church. Have the "keeper of the log" take notes to record what people say. One way to do this is to bring along copies of past church histories or annual reports. You want to remember what you have been doing that you should continue to do as a church.

In other words, start your reassessment of the church on the positive side. When we remember the past with thanksgiving, we may recall some of the stories and people that have made us what we are today. Try to distill the principles and values that stand behind these good memories. Why was Mr. Bennett such a good influence on the youth? Why was Mrs. Nestor's third grade class so memorable for so many children? What was it about the music ministry of Mrs. Kowalski that made such a difference in the lives of adults and children?

We cannot turn back the clock and relive a past moment in our church's history. But we can remember the underlying truths that made those times especially valuable. We also want to preserve what we value today. When churches consider changes in the way they go about ministry, I caution them not to throw out what has been good. It would be better to add something new to an existing ministry than to replace an old ministry completely.

For instance, many churches wonder if they should introduce new styles of music into their morning worship. I encourage them to keep one service the way it has been and then add a new service with a style that seeks to reach a new target audience. Add, don't take away. As we engage in conversation about what is valuable about the church's past and present, make a list of those attributes that should be conserved.

What Do We Need to Stop Doing?

Once we have taken stock of what we want to continue to be and do as a church, we need to turn the conversation toward what we should *stop doing*. There may be behaviors that we identify as dysfunctional that we need to learn how to stop. There may be programs or activities that have been in place for years that have outlived their usefulness. There may be positions and viewpoints we stand for that lead others to view us negatively.

Church researchers tell us that those outside of the Christian faith have very negative perceptions of Christianity. Much of the negativity is based on what Christians are perceived to do. So, the question of what we should *stop* doing takes on weightier significance these days. In chapter 6 we will turn our attention to ways in which we can strive to reach younger adults who, according to author David Kinnaman in *unChristian,* are particularly turned off.[1]

The information gathered in Ministry by Walking Around can be helpful here. We need to learn what the perceptions of us are from those in our community. We should particularly pay attention to what younger adults are saying about us. The key is to listen. Perception is not always reality. Nevertheless, it is important to hear what people say. We cannot be satisfied with superficial answers to the deep questions raised by what we should stop doing. At stake is the mission of the church for the day in which we live.

One dysfunction I have seen in mainline churches is the tendency toward negativity. It is typical of the inward-oriented church that seeks to satisfy self rather than be focused on the mission of God. When we express disappointment in the music of the service or the preaching of the pastor or the color of the rugs in the sanctuary, it sounds like whining.

Reverend Jim Downing, lead pastor of the First United Methodist Church in Sedalia, Missouri, spoke at a conference of church

1. See Kinnaman and Lyons, *unChristian,* 11.

leaders about the effect of such negativity. Jim said that one of the things that outsiders ask about church life is, "Is there infighting in the church?"[2]

It doesn't take a newcomer long to find out if there is infighting in the church. Sometimes it is downright obvious as when worship visitors overhear two people complaining in the pew ahead of them. Reverend Downing explained that there are three kinds of church people in relation to infighting.

There are *complainers* who tear down other people, including the pastor, without offering anything to build up. We need to declare to our churches: *The Complaint Department is closed!* There are *critics*. We can and should accommodate critics. Critics can be helpful when they offer solutions to the problem they see. What we really need are *champions*. Champions see an issue or problem and not only offer solutions, but they offer themselves as well to be instruments for the solution. They have a spirit that says "Yes" to what God can do in our midst.

We often joke that the seven last words of the church are "We never did it that way before." How different would it be if we remembered the *first seven words*: We can do all things in Christ (see Phil 4:13)?

For many churches, the first thing they need to stop doing is whining and complaining. Such behavior speaks poorly of the faith we have in Jesus Christ. It speaks poorly of our belief in the God who resurrects the dead. Along with Rev. Downing, we need to declare that the whining and complaint departments are closed. We should begin to make an attitude adjustment in our church. I like how one pastor approached this issue from the pulpit. She handed out rubber bracelets to everyone in the congregation. She invited her people to wear the bracelet as a reminder not to complain or whine for twenty-one straight days. If you can do it for that long it can become a habit, she reasoned. If someone found themselves complaining or whining, they had to switch the

2. Reverend Jim Downing, presentation at the National Gathering of United Methodist Congregational Developers, DoubleTree Hotel Houston Intercontinental Airport, Houston, Texas, February 29, 2008.

bracelet from one wrist to the other and start the twenty-one-day period all over again.

Whining and complaining are close relatives to *gossiping*, which the Bible rails against (see Prov 11:13; 2 Cor 12:20). These behaviors infuse a culture of negativity in the church that whittles away at hope. Newcomers pick up on such negativity quickly and soon find the exit door of the church. They are driven away by actions that fly in the face of the professed faith of a Christian.

As we travel the road to renewal, we need to be honest with ourselves about behaviors that reflect poorly on our faith in Christ. We need to seek attitude adjustments. Just as others will know we are disciples by our *love*, they will also know our negativity by our complaints, whining or gossip. Let's commit to eradicate these ungodly behaviors from our community of faith.

We also need to stop doing activities or events that have lost their meaning or usefulness. One church had scheduled a fish and chips dinner two times a year for as long as anyone could remember. The dinners raised important funds for the mission of the church. Members became tired if not bored by the same old, same old, year in and year out. Someone finally asked why the church continued to do this. While there were some who remembered how much fun it had been to work together in an event like this, most admitted that it had become drudgery and the fundraiser had lost its focus and meaning. Before thinking of alternatives, the church decided to stop doing fish and chips dinners.

The decision led others to ask the question, "What else should we *stop* doing?" A lively discussion ensued in which church leaders reviewed all the programs and activities of the church asking whether they should continue doing them or stop doing them.

What Are We Not Doing That We Should Start Doing?

Once we have gained clarity about what we value and celebrate as a community of faith and once we have reflected on what we need to stop doing, we can begin to think and dream about what

God is calling us to *start* doing. It is important that we follow the sequential process here. If we have named the positive behaviors we celebrate and identified the dysfunctional behaviors and actions we want to stop, it should lead logically to new behaviors and actions to start.

One church articulated a mission statement that called them to "make disciples of Jesus Christ." No one argued with this statement. However, as they participated in discussing reassessment of their ministry, one leader asked, "What kind of disciples are we?" Are we living out Christian discipleship that is worth emulating? This question goes to the heart of a focus that is both inward and outward at the same time. While we want an outward-oriented mission as a church that invites others to become disciples of Jesus Christ, at the same time we need to reflect on the kind of discipleship already present. We need to focus inwardly and ask challenging questions about the quality of our own discipleship.

There are excellent tools to help a church take a look at itself. Discipleship Ministries' Junius Dotson recently wrote a guide for developing a discipleship system in local congregations. This guide addresses the "why" for being a disciple and brings clarity on how to make disciples. The initiative is known for its hashtag: #SeeAll-ThePeople. Natural Church Development (NCD) is an approach to ministry that holds a mirror up to the congregation to see how it measures up to eight quality characteristics of the church. Christian A. Schwartz, a German Protestant Christian and the founder of NCD, has developed a survey instrument to measure church health. Survey results will identify what a church needs to work on in order to becoming healthier and thereby release the potential for growth.[3]

Another tool to help a church reassess its ministry is the "Readiness 360" that can be accessed online.[4] Developed as a partnership between Christie Latona and Paul Nixon, Readiness 360 helps measure the relationships in a congregation and its readiness

3. For more information about Natural Church Development, go to http://www.ncd-international.org/public/.

4. See http://readiness360.org/ for more information.

to multiply its ministry. Now administered by the Reverend Dr. Phil Maynard, a church consultant and coach, this instrument will help a church take stock of its current reality and plan for the future. The website gives the rationale for its use:

> In this dynamic era, churches need nimble leadership and cultural readiness in order to maximize their impact and blessing on the world as followers of Jesus Christ. It is not enough to "grow the church." We need to multiply ministry. We believe that any church can reclaim the foundational multiplication DNA of the Jesus movement. *Readiness 360* embodies the belief that the most fruitful church multiplication efforts come from healthy congregations with strong leadership, spiritual intensity, dynamic relationships, missional alignment and cultural openness. By taking our exclusive 360-degree assessment, any church can now evaluate the behaviors, patterns, and attitudes that contribute to success or failure when developing new places for new people or stepping out in bold risk-taking mission.[5]

The key to reassessment lies in a church's willingness to be honest with itself. How can we pretend to "Make Disciples of Jesus Christ" of others when our own discipleship lacks vitality? Whether we use a tool like Natural Church Development or Readiness 360, or whether we ask questions on our own, we need to reassess the quality and health of ourselves as disciples of Jesus Christ. The question that asks, "What are we not doing and should start doing" begins with an assessment of our discipleship behaviors.

Once we reassess our behaviors, we can look to the programs and activities that could support the kinds of Christian behaviors we want to live as disciples.

I consulted with a church that confessed that the majority of the members did not pray or read the Bible regularly. They said that they did not have enough time. Life was so busy and hectic that they never found the quiet time to read the Bible or pray. As I worked with this congregation we tried to articulate questions that

5. See http://readiness360.org/about/.

addressed the underlying issues that led to tension between time and prayer.

We asked, what is the meaning of prayer? What is the meaning of time in today's cultural context? Is time something to be filled? By saying we don't have time to pray or read the Bible, what are we afraid of? What are we escaping from? If we were to slow things down enough to pray or read the Bible, what would we be missing?

As we discussed the answers to these questions, we began to do the work of reassessment. Too often we do not take the time to ask the "why" questions that help us explore the reasons behind our behaviors and actions. The work of reassessing our ministry lies in asking these questions and not being satisfied with superficial or easy answers.

What are we not doing that we should start doing? Once we identify what is lacking in our witness as disciples, we can begin to list action steps to help us move to a better place of discipleship.

Identifying the Key Issues

Reassessing our ministry helps us address the issues we face as a congregation. As we travel the road to renewal we want to know the challenges we face on the way, the condition of the vehicle, the amount of gas in the tank, and weather conditions. Similarly, as we seek to rediscover the church's mission, we need to know its present state.

Renewal starts with identification of key issues. We need to know what we need to work on before we can pretend to improve. It is not enough to know the symptoms that cause disease. If a person is to become healthy, he or she needs to correct the causes that bring on illness. The key issues in renewal are the obstacles in our pathway that prevent us from moving toward a greater degree of health and well-being as a congregation.

As you reflect on the celebrations of ministry and everything that is good and positive about your church, formulate a list of the basic values that characterize who you are as a community of faith. As you reflect on the behaviors and activities that need to be stopped as well as the ones that need to be started, begin to identify themes and issues that emerge.

Core Values

Core values have to do with what we believe to be true and what we act upon as a result of beliefs. In the process of reassessing the mission and ministry of the church, you will want to clarify your core values. For example, United Methodists have always been known to value relationships with other Christians and so have championed cooperation with other churches. A core belief of the United Methodist Church is ecumenism. An action that results from such a belief is in involvement in ecumenical organizations such as an Inter-religious Fellowship for the Homeless.

Another core value for United Methodists, historically, has been strong support for education. The Methodist movement in eighteenth-century England was born in a university. The value of proper training, both formal and informal, has always been part of the DNA of people called Methodists. Over the years in the United States more than seventy colleges and universities were founded by United Methodists. Ecumenism and education have been core values.

United Methodists have also stressed personal and social holiness. From the days of Wesley, people called Methodists have encouraged a sanctified life manifested in living out the means of grace. Wesley understood these means as including both works of piety and works of mercy.

Works of piety include prayer, Bible reading, partaking of Holy Communion, fasting, holy conferencing (meeting together with other Christians), and healthy living. Works of mercy include doing good, visiting the sick, visiting the imprisoned, feeding and clothing those in need, giving generously what one has earned, and seeking justice. As an example of the latter, Wesley sought redressing the social evil of slavery in his day. The last letter he wrote, just days before he died at the age of eighty-eight, was directed to

William Wilberforce, a member of Parliament, encouraging him in his fight to eradicate slavery from the British Empire. These means of grace have become core values for United Methodists through the ages.

It is important for each local church to articulate its core values. These values should draw from the historical tradition of its denomination, and they should also reflect the particular setting of its mission and ministry.

When United Methodists began to start new churches in Honduras in 1998, the leaders articulated a list of core values that formed the foundation of their work. These included scriptural mandates for mission engagement, valuing the people to be engaged in mission and their cultural heritage, the Wesleyan heritage, commitment to ecumenism, commitment to historical partnerships in the region, connection with worldwide Methodism, and commitment to the goals of Global Ministries of The United Methodist Church.

The core values of a church help define its theology of mission engagement. When it comes time to articulate your vision and mission, the core values provide a reference point. You will want to align your vision and mission statements with your core values. Making a list of core values, as part of the process of reassessing the church's ministry, will become foundational for later work on vision and mission statements and putting together a Ministry Action Plan (MAP).

A university town church took the Natural Church Development survey to reassess their ministry. Survey results indicated that lack of evangelism (needs-based evangelism) was holding them back from achieving a greater measure of health. Many of the leaders did not like the term itself. They recalled negative experiences with evangelists who had invaded privacy and sought to avoid this ministry area altogether. They remembered a core value that came from one of Wesley's simple rules: do no harm. Their negative experiences with evangelism were times when this rule was violated. They did not want to partake of a ministry action plan that would in any way do harm to others.

As they explored more deeply the meaning of evangelism, understanding core values helped them reshape their ministry. They discovered that "evangelism" had less to do with their own negative experiences and more with hospitality and faith sharing in positive ways. They identified key issues they needed to address while holding onto their core values. These included greater attention to hospitality ministry, an adequate discipleship system in the church that helped members and newcomers alike deepen their spirituality, and ways to help one another share their faith stories with others. As they identified the key issues, "evangelism" no longer scared them away from engaging in the important ministry of sharing the good news of Christ with others.

Articulating core values helps the church formulate the ground rules for corporate behavior. It is a key ingredient for the reassessment of ministry and helps the church gain clarity as to where God wants it to go to gain a greater measure of health. Reassessment serves as a marker on the road to renewal that gives us confidence that indeed, we are going in the right direction and that God has something very special in store for us as we continue on the way.

Your Turn

1. What are you doing in the church that you should continue to do? Why are these behavior and actions valuable?

2. What behaviors of the church should you stop doing? Review the programs and activities of your church. Which ones need to be stopped? Why?

3. What are you not doing now that you should start doing? Begin to look at behaviors that manifest discipleship and then move to actions you can take to arrive at a healthier place.

4. Name 3–5 key issues that need to be addressed in your church for you to realize the mission God has prepared for you to do.

5. Make a list of the core values that your church holds dear. Draw upon the historical tradition of your denomination and the particular context of your place of ministry.

5

Road Break

WHEN ON A ROAD trip, sometimes you have to stop, get out, and stretch. You need a break from driving.

Once I traveled across the United States, from New Jersey to California and back, with three friends. We wanted to make as much progress as we could and created a rotation system where two of us were awake while two others slept. We stopped for a combination bathroom break and gas fill-up about every two or three hours and managed to reach Denver, Colorado, in thirty hours. Then, we slowed things down to take in the grandeur of the Rockies and beyond.

On a Sunday morning near Sacramento, California, we broke camp early and headed to church. The service, while similar in many ways to what we experienced in New Jersey, included some elements that were new to us. They placed a "Welcome Table" in the fellowship room adjacent to the sanctuary. The worship bulletin invited first-time visitors to visit the table to obtain a welcome gift. At the table we filled out an information card giving our contact information and each of us received a bag filled with homemade baked goodies, a coffee mug and a brochure with information about the church. Attached to the brochure was a Starbucks gift card. Since we each received a "Welcome Bag" we enjoyed the goodies the next day of traveling and had a latte at one of the many Starbucks on the way. We were able to talk with members of the church after the service. The people we met exuded a friendly and open hospitality and we took special notice. We asked ourselves how we could incorporate the same spirit of authentic welcoming into our church back east. When we arrived home from our trip, there were handwritten letters from the church thanking us for having worshipped with them.

As you travel the road to renewal with your leadership team, plan to take some breaks along the way to learn from other churches. The break will offer rest from the road and allow you to see church from a different perspective. The idea is not to imitate what another church does, but to recognize the principles behind what they do and apply the same principles to your specific setting.

In Sacramento, we experienced great hospitality by the local church we visited. The question for us was not to imitate what we saw, but to ask the question, "What would great hospitality look like back in New Jersey?" We may go to Dunkin' Donuts rather than Starbucks. Perhaps we could come up with a different idea altogether as we imagine what radical hospitality would look like at home. The important takeaway from our visit was to apply the principles that underlay the special experience we had.

We discussed among ourselves as we ate the cookies what a warm, hospitable welcome would look like in New Jersey. Would we include a gift card to Dunkin' Donuts? How could we make it fit with our local likes? These are the questions coming from a "road break."

Find a church to visit where the vitality and health of the congregation are creating a buzz. Your denominational executive may have some ideas. You could also ask folk in your own congregation. Often people visit other churches to attend baptisms or confirmations or are visiting relatives. Ask people where they have seen a healthy, vibrant community of faith in action. You may have to take a detour from your road to renewal to spend time on such visits. Include the pastor on the road break. Ask someone else to fill the pulpit on a given Sunday and take the team, including the pastor, to another church.

You will get even more out of your experience if you make arrangements with the church you are visiting ahead of time. Ask leaders of that church to meet with you after worship. Take them out to lunch and ask them questions about how his or her church arrived at such a vibrant type of ministry. Ask questions that help uncover the principles behind what they do. You don't want to imitate what another church does, but you do want to learn the principles and discuss how these can be transferred to your situation.

Each summer Global Ministries, Discipleship Ministries, and Path 1 of the United Methodist Church sponsor a School of Congregational Development.[1] The school starts on a Thursday and ends on Saturday. On the Sunday immediately after, participants are encouraged to go on their own "road break" by making visits to churches in the area. Participants sign up ahead of time for one of the dozen or more churches to visit. Buses line up on Sunday morning to take people to any one among a dozen congregations. After worship, the visiting people from the School have lunch at the church and listen to laity and clergy from that church tell their story. This experience provides an excellent opportunity to see what others are doing to create vibrant, healthy congregations.

Churches today are learning more and more about how to be hospitable to newcomers. This past year I focused my road break visits to churches that practice winsome hospitality. I was impressed with Ginghamsburg Church's "five-touch rule." Ginghamsburg Church is located in Tipp City, Ohio, and has grown from a small, family-size congregation to one of the largest in the denomination over the past thirty years. From the time I parked my car in the parking lot until I sat down in worship five different people shook my hand and personally greeted me. Today's churches are searching for ways to go beyond mere friendliness to creating opportunities where true friendships can form.

My mother taught me a lasting lesson on the difference between friendliness and making friends. She and Dad had to move over ten times during their first twelve years of marriage. My father

---

1. For information related to the School of Congregational Development, see http://www.umcdiscipleship.org/.

was a salesman and the companies he worked for were constantly assigning him to new places. On the occasion of Mom's ninety-fourth birthday, my sister and I asked her how she had managed to pick up everything and move with a family of five to a new town or city where she didn't know a soul. "I would find a Methodist church," she replied, "because there I knew I could make a friend."

I thought it interesting how she worded her response. She didn't look for a "friendly church," but rather a church where she could make a friend. There is a big difference. The difference was underscored for me recently upon hearing of a colleague who moved to a new town and sought out the closest United Methodist church.

In the case of my colleague, he found a "friendly church." People were kind. They smiled at him. Some greeted him during the after-worship fellowship hour. But, he wasn't making any friends. He even went so far as to invite some of the church members he met to his home—to try to build a relationship—but they couldn't find the time to come over. My colleague had found a friendly church, but not one where he could make a friend. He has given up trying and now is attending a church of another denomination where within two weeks of his first visit he was invited over to a member's house for dinner. That was what my mother had experienced years before. Being a newcomer, she needed to make friends. She needed someone who would invite her and my dad over for fellowship. A "friendly church" was not good enough. She needed a church where she could make a friend.

People long to be connected to community. They need to make friends where fellowship can be taken to a deeper level. Many churches have systems in place to meet these needs. They are intentional about inviting newcomers to join small groups.

In my road break visits over the past year, I wanted to *learn how churches moved newcomers from interest to involvement.* I wanted to learn how the churches in my area of the world could do a better job of hospitality that would go beyond friendliness. The first thing I learned from my visits to churches that did this well was that we need to acknowledge that the responsibility for making newcomers feel welcomed and loved resides with us—the church—and not with the newcomer. My colleague should not have had to invite members to his house. Members of the church he was visiting should have gone out of their way to invite him to theirs. That he moved on to another church speaks to the failing of the church he left and not anything he did or did not do.

I learned five simple steps from my visits to churches that should help any church move a newcomer from interest to involvement. *First, help the newcomer form relationships with other members.* Don't let her get away from fellowship hour without introducing her to one or two members of the church. *Second, help the newcomer find a place in a small group,* be it the choir, a Sunday School class, or a women's fellowship circle. *Third, help foster friendships for the newcomer.* Make time to invite her to dinner at your house along with her spouse or significant other, or to join an existing friendship group of the church on an outing. *Fourth, help provide opportunities for newcomers to grow in their faith by getting involved in some form of Christian service.* Does your church have a ministry of outreach or does it take a volunteer mission trip somewhere? Invite the newcomer along! While they engage in meaningful Christian service they will also deepen their relationships with fellow members of the church. *Finally, help provide opportunities for newcomers to grow as disciples of Jesus Christ.* Once the newcomer is involved in the life of the church, create a system whereby she is the point person for newer newcomers. In this way they multiply the blessing they received and learn to disciple others.

The fruit of my road break visits to find a hospitable church resonated with the lessons I learned from my mother. There is a huge difference between a "friendly church" and a church where you can make a friend. It's a lesson that our churches need to remember.

Research

There are other ways to take road breaks. Assign a team member to do research. From the discovery made through reassessing your ministry, research the Internet for ways to address the issues identified. Canvass the websites of churches known for their vitality. Enter key words related to the issues you want to address in your web browser search engine. For instance, a church that wants to strengthen its "hospitality ministry" might enter those words in a search engine. Take the time to scan through the entries and come up with a list of ideas. Again, the idea is not to imitate what another church has done, but rather apply the principles to your setting.

At a university town church, new students who visited in September received a special hospitality packet that included homemade cookies. The church asked what welcoming hospitality in a university setting would look like. Throughout the semester the church provided care packages to students filled with cards of encouragement as well as homemade goodies. Welcoming hospitality in another context would look different. Each church needs to discover how to apply the principles behind their actions to their particular situation.

In addition to Web-based research, assign someone from the team to investigate other ways to address the issues. Invite a congregational vitality coach to your church and ask what tools of ministry he recommends to help a church gain a greater measure of health. Find out what resources he recommends that a church could explore. Some will point in the direction of congregational surveys, demographic analysis, or ways to track trends in the culture.

Search the blogosphere for discussion threads that address issues similar to what you have identified. Or start your own discussion thread.

Reading

There are many provocative books that will open eyes and minds to new ways of thinking about the church. If a church is interested in analyzing why younger people are not attracted to its services, books such as *unChristian* or George Barna and David Kinnaman's *Churchless: Understanding Today's Unchurched and How to Connect with Them* can help stimulate dialogue. If a church is seeking ways to meet people outside the walls of the church, read Neil Cole's *Organic Church*, or Leonard Sweet's *The Gospel according to Starbucks*. To gain a greater understanding of the paradigm shifts that are occurring in our larger culture and how it affects church life, read *Weird Church: Welcome to the Twenty-First Century*, by Beth Estock and Paul Nixon, or *Flipping Church*, edited by Michael Baughman. For ways to reach out to the community, read my book *A Missionary Mindset: What Church Leaders Need to Know to Reach Their Community—Lessons from E. Stanley Jones.* There are many other books out there to stimulate reflection. Assign several team members to read the same book and brief the team on its contents. Prepare provocative questions from the ideas in the books to lead the team in discussion.

Bishop Sudarshana Devadhar of the New England Annual Conference of The United Methodist Church encourages churches to read and discuss particular books as a means to take a road break from normal activities. Each year he suggests books to stimulate dialogue about the way in which the church engages ministry. Some of his recommendations have included *Building a Discipling Culture*, by Mike Breen and Steve Cockram; *Spiritual Kaizen*, by Grant Hagiya; and *Seven Levers*, by Robert Schnase. At times he has received letters critical of the choices while at other times church folk have expressed the great blessings of reading the books. Regardless of their reaction, the bishop is grateful that churches have taken him up on the challenge of reading the books and dialoguing about them. The time taken to reflect and dialogue about the ideas have enriched the churches and led them to seek other ways in which they could rediscover the church's mission.

Taking a break is important as we travel along the road to renewal. We need to get out of our own routines by visiting other churches, finding out what other Christian communities are doing to bring healthy, vital ministry into their midst and to read books together to stimulate thinking about ways in which to present the gospel message in today's world.

Your Turn

Do some research on how other congregations have responded to the challenge of making connections between church and community. Visit a church that has excelled in reaching out to its community. Denominational leaders can help you discover where to go. Set up the visit ahead of time. Send at least five people from your leadership team. As you worship and dialogue with the host church, make notes to bring back to the larger team.

1. Describe what it was like to visit the church. How were you welcomed? Did you feel at home? What were the principles behind the way in which you were greeted?

2. How was worship similar or different from the way you worship at your church?

3. How did the church move from where they were to where they are now? What bumps on the road did they experience? If they had to do it all over, what mistakes would they like to avoid?

4. Assign someone to research issues that you identified in previous sessions and have him or her report learnings back to the team.

5. What are some of the ways your church could practice a deeper form of hospitality?

6. Decide on a book to read as a group and dedicate a session to the discussion of the book. Look for a book that helps address the issues you identified in previous sessions.

6

Reaching Younger People

Lovett Weems, of the Lewis Center for Church Leadership, urges mainline churches to reach more people, younger people and people with more diverse backgrounds.[1] As we seek to make connections with the community in which God has placed us, we need to articulate a vision for the future that comes from conversations with younger people that live in our midst.

This is a problem for many US churches. Recent books mentioned in chapter 5 allude to the difficulty (*UnChristian* and *Churchless*). Another book, written by Robert Wuthnow, Andlinger Professor of Sociology and director of the Center for the Study of Religion at Princeton University, goes into detail about the disconnect between mainline Protestant churches and younger generations. In *After the Baby Boomers*, Wuthnow brings together social science research and theology to try to explain why the generations that have come after the baby boomers are largely missing from church. Wuthnow avoids popular generational labels like "Generation X" or "Generation Y" or "Busters" or "Millennials" to describe this group. He prefers to call them "younger adults."[2]

Wuthnow points to the fact that young adults today marry later and have children later than previous generations. They take longer to establish themselves in careers and settle into a

1. See Weems, "Leadership for Reaching Emerging Generations," 6.
2. Wuthnow, *After the Baby Boomers*, 2.

community. Churches geared to developmental stages of early adulthood find these stages occurring later (chronologically) in younger people's lives. "More Americans are coming of age at forty than ever before." Wuthnow writes of the relevance of these understandings of young adulthood to the church:

> Congregations *could* be a valuable source of support for young adults. They *could* be places where young adults gravitate to talk about the difficult decisions they are facing or to meet other people of the same age. Congregations *could* be guiding the career decisions of younger adults or helping them think about their budgets and their personal priorities. But . . . this potential is often going unrealized. It will continue to go unrealized as long as congregations invest in youth programs for high school students and assume this is enough. It will also go unrealized if congregational leaders focus on their graying memberships and do not look more creatively to the future.[3]

Wuthnow uses the word "tinkering" to describe young adults' approach to religion and spirituality. "They do not rely on only one way of doing things." The key to understanding the tinkerer is *uncertainty*.[4]

A challenge for our churches today is to address the uncertainty that many younger adults experience. Before we can address those issues, however, we need to learn to engage younger adults in conversation. This is especially important given the generation gap that exists among many of our churches.

I have had the privilege of visiting many churches across our connection, from the East Coast to the West: from Florida to Maine, Minnesota to Mississippi, New Mexico to the Pacific Northwest. Many are beacons of light for their communities: thriving congregations, healthy in every way, serving to help transform lives and communities. Some are hanging in there, keeping the

3. Ibid., 12.
4. Ibid., 13.

faith and keeping the doors open for the sake of the gospel. And some are far from thriving—they are surviving.

As one privileged to visit so many churches, there is one unmistakable reality: United Methodist congregations tend to be made up of older people. There is an age gap. For instance, the average age of a United Methodist in New Jersey is fifty-seven, while the average age of someone living in New Jersey is thirty-seven. Unless our churches find intentional ways to reach out to younger generations, that age gap will only widen in the future.

My colleague Craig Miller, who serves as Director of Pastoral Leadership at Discipleship Ministries, has researched this generation gap. According to Miller, churches today "will flourish or flounder depending on their ability to be in ministry to new people groups," including those from the so-called postmodern generations.[5]

There are two generations of people that are largely missing from United Methodist churches (and other mainline churches): these are the so-called Gen Xers, born between 1965 and 1981, and the Millennials, born from 1982 to 1999. Together they comprise what many call the postmoderns or what Wuthnow prefers to refer to simply as "younger adults." The worldview of these people is very different from my own. I am part of the baby boom generation that dominated the cultural landscape from the 1960s through the 1990s.

Postmodern is an expression that has been bantered around for some time now. It is important to remember that the prefix post does not mean anti. It means emerging from. It is at once rooted in the worldview of the past and at the same time emerging from that worldview. It carries the past with itself and it experiences life in ways that are radically different from those of us who are older. Some people point to the fall of the Berlin Wall in 1989 as a symbolic ending of the modern age. This was the age when human reason was to find solutions for the entire world's problems. Emerging out of modernity means that the idea that humans can

5. Miller, *Next Church.Now*, 37.

solve the world's problems may not be the final answer. There is a yearning for something more.

One of the signs of this postmodern era is an increase in attention to matters spiritual. We see it in books sold that deal with religious and spiritual subjects. Books like Rick Warren's *The Purpose Driven Life*, which has sold more than thirty-two million copies. Books like *The Da Vinci Code*, which continues to break records for works of fiction. Books like the *Left Behind* series, and books that address issues such as meditation, prayer, and ultimate meaning. There seems to be a hunger for spirituality today.

And yet two generations of people are largely missing from our churches, which have specialized in providing religious and spiritual answers. Why is there such a disconnect?

The Millennial generation especially will mark the tempo of the next twenty years. They are large in number and will dominate the cultural scene, much like we baby boomers dominated culture up through the 1990s. Millennials have grown up amid great diversity. About 35 percent experienced their parents' divorce. Eighteen percent have been raised by an unmarried parent. The concept of family will have more to do with relationship than with biology for this generation. This generation, more than any before, will have to deal with the radical revolution brought on by information technology.[6]

Think about how technology continues to change our world. I can remember not too long ago, say the early 1990s, trying to convince my church that it should buy a computer. People twenty-five and younger have never known a world without personal computers.

According to Craig Miller, the greatest danger that Millennials will face has to do with the attitude of previous generations, who may view them as the enemy rather than as a generation who needs support and guidance. The danger is that those of us who are older will be asking "what can be done *about* this new generation, instead of what can be done *for* and *with* them."[7]

6. Ibid., 38–42.
7. Ibid., 42.

I believe that the postmodern generations are part of a different culture than the one I have known in my lifetime. I struggle to understand their culture. The Bible is a resource for the community of faith. We turn to the pages of the Bible to gain insight into our human condition. I draw your attention to a passage that comes from Paul's letter to the Galatians. The second chapter deals with a confrontation between Peter and Paul. It was a crucial problem and if we learn its lessons we may gain insight on how to approach the missing generations of our church.

The problem that Peter and Paul disagreed about had to do with the inclusivity of the church. Do converts from outside of the Jewish religion need to observe the Jewish law upon receiving Christ? In other words, would a Christian first have to become a Jew in order to be a faithful follower of Jesus?

There were many in the church who insisted on the observance of Jewish law. These people were known as the Judaizers. There were others, like Paul, who were convinced that in Jesus, new ground was broken in the relationship between God and humanity. Paul argued that salvation cannot be earned by legal observance, by works, by anything that we humans do to prove our worthiness. For Paul, salvation (and by salvation we mean being put right with God) is a gift given freely by God for those who deposit their faith and trust in him.

The conflict came to a head at the first grand council of the church, which was held in Jerusalem. Among those present was Peter, the most intimate disciple of Jesus, the rock upon which the church was to be built. The delegation at the council was mixed between those who had been Jews and those who had been Gentiles. In this mixed company, Peter insisted on observing Jewish law: the ritual washings before eating, the restrictions on certain foods.

Paul saw that action as sending the wrong message and he was incensed. For Paul, nothing less than the mission and future of the church was at stake. Would the non-Jewish followers of Jesus be made to feel like second-class citizens because they did not observe the Jewish law? Would the followers of Jesus end up forming a small, insignificant sect within the Jewish religion or would they form a universal community of believers, reaching to save all humankind for all time?

Paul Johnson is a British author of more than fifty books. His *History of Christianity* begins with this incident between Peter and Paul. If Peter had prevailed, Johnson intimates, he would not be writing the book. If Peter had prevailed, we would not be discussing these matters today.[8]

God worked through the council and through Paul. Paul had been steeped in Jewish law. He knew exactly what he was talking about when he insisted on including non-Jews in the church in such a way that they did not have to first conform to the cultural and ritualistic behaviors of Jews.

He spoke directly to Peter. Listen to the words from his letter to the Galatians: "When Peter came to Antioch, I opposed him in public, because he was clearly wrong." I like Eugene Peterson's rendering in *The Message*: "When Peter came to Antioch, I had a face-to-face confrontation with him because he was clearly out of line." This was no private matter. The future of the church depended on the issue. Paul calls Peter a coward, as someone not walking a straight path in line with the truth of the gospel.

The next little segment in Paul's letter to the Galatians is commonly referred to as Paul's Gospel. It follows in his opposition to Judaizers. "We know," Paul wrote, "that a man is put right with God only through faith in Jesus Christ, never by doing what the Law requires. . . . So far as the Law is concerned . . . I am dead, killed by the Law itself in order that I might live for God. I have been put to death with Christ on his cross . . ." And here comes that most beautiful of affirmations: "So that it is no longer I who live, but it is Christ who lives in me" (Gal 2:20).

Should postmodern people, the younger generations that Robert Wuthnow refers to as "younger adults," be given the chance to practice Christian faith *as* postmoderns, or must they first be converted into modern Christianity? What if the gospel needs to be incarnated into the emerging postmodern culture, just as it was within ancient, medieval, and modern cultures?

8. Johnson, *History of Christianity*, 3–6.

We should ask ourselves, do younger people first have to embrace the form and style of Christian worship the way we older adults practice it or can they approach the gospel with new forms of liturgy and music that speak to their generation? Moreover, are we open to accompanying younger adults in their discovery of the gospel?

It may take a "missionary mindset" on the part of us older adults to reach younger adults. Just as a missionary learns the nuances of the culture he or she engages, we, too, need to learn the culture of younger adults today. Just as Paul learned to become a Jew, in order to win Jews and to become all things to all people for the sake of the gospel, are not we, older adults, challenged to understand and embrace ways to reach younger adults?

For Paul, there is something greater than the law, there is something greater than observing religious ritual, there is something greater than holding fast to a particular style of worship: there is life lived in the Spirit of Jesus Christ. We turn now to a pertinent question. How can our churches thrive in the future by reaching the postmodern generations?

We are invited to have the heart of God. Remember the familiar Bible passage sometimes referred to as the gospel in miniature: "God so loved the world that he gave his only Son, so that everyone who believes in him may not perish but may have eternal life" (John 3:16). It doesn't say God so loved the church. It doesn't say God so loved The United Methodist Church. It says, "God so loved *the world*": humanity, people, all people, including the postmodern generation. The invitation of the gospel is to *open our hearts* to postmoderns. Love them. We are invited to love the world, just as God loves the world. We do this by listening, understanding, engaging, dialoguing.

We are invited to have the mind of the Apostle Paul. Recognize that postmoderns are people of a different culture than what many of us experience. We need to find ways to bring them to the table without requiring them to first be like us. We need to *open our minds* to dialogue with them, strive to understand what is different about their worldview and invite them to come to the depth and breadth of Christian community. Build bridges of love and understanding and work with these generations to discover what it means to follow Jesus, to worship God and be a community of faith in this postmodern age.

Several years ago, I had the privilege of co-teaching a course on Evangelism with Bishop Sudarshana Devadhar at Drew Theological School. I was impressed with the caliber of students. Many are young people in the generations that are missing from our churches: students who are twenty-three, twenty-four years old, responding to the call of God to be in ministry. I talked to one twenty-three-year-old student who envisioned a church filled with persons from his generation. He envisioned a church that honors the best of our tradition but at the same time involves people in worship in radically participatory ways.

My conversation with him filled me with hope. It will be his generation that will carry the torch of the church into the future. The challenge for those of us who are older is to work *with them*, not against them. Let's not require that they be like us before they fully embrace what it means to follow Jesus in today's world.

We are invited to open our doors to Jesus in new ways. Remember the passage from the book of Revelation. "Listen, I am standing at the door, knocking; if you hear my voice and open the door, I will come in to you and eat with you, and you with me" (Rev 3:20). Jesus wants us to open our doors to him and Jesus wants those of us inside the church to open our doors to those who are outside.

Cuban Methodists were forced to open their doors in new ways in the wake of the revolution that occurred in the 1960s. In the mid-sixties, in the revolution's first years, the Methodist Church lost sixty-four out of seventy of its pastors. They left the country. So did many laity. The one hundred churches in the country ended up with a combined average worship attendance of one thousand, or ten per church. Something had to be done.

The leaders who were left in Cuba decided to focus their resources and energies on the children and youth of the country. They knew that if they did not teach them about Jesus, they would never learn of him. When they began reaching out to youth and children, they discovered that they had to make some changes in order for them to hear the gospel. They worked with the youth and soon began singing songs that the youth suggested. They changed their liturgy.

Slowly the emphasis on youth began to produce change. The young people began to come to church to learn about the Bible. Through the church and with permission of the US government, I have had the opportunity to visit Cuban Methodists on four different occasions. When I visited several years ago, instead of one thousand in worship there were eighty-five thousand. Now there are more than two hundred churches. The church reinvented itself as it sought to be faithful to God in reaching a new generation of people.

Lovett Weems challenges us to reach more people, younger people, and more diverse people with the gospel of Jesus Christ. A critical issue for churches embarking on the road to renewal is how they will engage younger generations. Nothing less than the future of the church is at stake.

Your Turn

1. What is the average age of your congregation?

2. What generations are missing from your church?

3. What can you do to begin new conversations with younger adults?

4. How can a "missionary mindset" help you cross the culture divide to reach younger adults?

7

Roadmaps Start with Vision

THE BOOK OF JEREMIAH includes words of hope for the people of
Israel living in exile in Babylonia. Jeremiah says that God wants
the people to move forward with their lives, bearing sons and
daughters and seeking the welfare of the city in which they lived.
In due time, God will bring his people back to the promised land.
For now, they need to take stock of their current reality and live in
faith and hope. "For surely I know the plans I have for you, says
the Lord, plans for your welfare and not for your harm, to give you
a future with hope" (Jer 29:11). God has a plan for today's church.
God has a plan for your local church.

Like the Israelites living in exile, today's current reality may
seem foreign to many in the church. Perhaps our paradigm of the
church was shaped by a previous era (i.e., the 1950s) and we sense
that what worked then does not necessarily work today. The work
of articulating a roadmap to renewal is in recognizing God's plan
and writing it down.

On our trip so far, we have sought to reconnect to God
through prayer and understanding our witness. We have rediscov-
ered the landscape of our parish area by looking at demographics
and talking with people who are not yet part of our community
of faith to gain perspective on the perception those outside of the
church have as well as the perception of needs in the community.
We have analyzed our ministry, clarifying core values and what we

want to continue as well as identifying what needs to change. We have taken road breaks to visit other churches to learn the under-lying principles that make them vital congregations.

Now we are ready to put together a Ministry Action Plan (or MAP) that seeks to be in alignment with our core values and the plans God has for our church, plans to give us a future with hope.

All the discussions held so far on the road come to fruition in the articulation of a plan that we believe is God inspired and God directed. We start with vision and mission and then work on articulating goals and objectives that are part of the MAP—the roadmap that the church will follow into the future.

There are many ways in which a church can work the process of strategic planning. As we begin this part of the road to renewal, it is important to outline and define what lies ahead. In chapter 4 (Reassess) we began the work by defining *core values* and identi-fying *key issues* that the church needs to address. From there we articulate a *vision*.

Vision has to do with the larger purpose of what it means to be a church. It responds to the question, why do we exist? A vision statement articulates what God envisions our church to be in the particular setting in which God has placed us.

Here are some sample vision statements from the world of business:[1]

- Wal-Mart (1990): "Become a $125 billion company by the year 2000"
- Sony (1950s): "Become the company most known for chang-ing the worldwide poor-quality image of Japanese products"
- Boeing (1950): "Become the dominant player in commercial aircraft and bring the world into the jet age"
- Ford Motor Company (early 1900s): "Ford will democratize the automobile"

1. http://www.family-business-experts.com/sample-mission-statements.html.

All of these statements make reference to what the company is called *to be*.

The next step in the process is *Mission*. Here we attempt to answer the question, what are we called *to do*? More precisely, what has God called the church to do in response to the vision we discern from God. The mission of the church can change as our surrounding context changes. Whereas the vision of the church is more of a constant, the mission of the church changes direction or emphasis given the challenges of a specific time, culture and set of circumstances. For instance, many churches are in communities with changing demographics. New populations of people are moving in. How will the church respond? While God may continue to call us to a vision of serving as a sign, preview and instrument of the reign of God, what are we called *to do* with new people groups moving into our community? How are we to live out the vision God has called us to in a changing context?

The next step in the process is to set *goals and objectives*. Goals are measurable indicators of what we are trying to accomplish. An example of a goal statement is: By the end of the present five-year period, our church will have twice as many people volunteering in the local Habit for Humanity project. This is measurable. You will know at the end of five years whether or not you have reached the goal. Objectives are the actions steps that we undertake to achieve our goals.

The church then needs to map out its strategy for *evaluating* its plan. How will we stay on course? When will we know that we are effective? Who is responsible for seeing that goals and objectives are met? How will we monitor the effectiveness of our plan?

The steps in the planning process are: core values, key issues, vision, mission, goals and objectives, and evaluation. We turn now to the task of putting together a Ministry Action Plan (MAP) that will clarify our direction for the near future. This MAP will chart our course for the next three to five years. The following chart shows each step in the creation of our MAP.

A Design for a Process to Create a Ministry Action Plan (MAP)

STEPS IN THE PROCESS	Define Core Values (What are the essentials of our beliefs?)	Diagnose Present Situation (Where are we now?)	Discern Vision (What are we called to be?)	Describe Mission (What are we called to do?)	Determine Goals and Objectives (What are the measurable goals and action steps needed to live out what we are called to be and do?)	Delineate Roadmarks (How will we know we have reached our goals and objectives?)
	Core Value #1	Issue #1	Called to be … #1	Called to do … #1	Goals 1–3	Roadmarker #1
	Core Value #2					
	Core Value #3	Issue #2	Called to be … #2	Called to do … #2	Objectives 1–3	Roadmarker #2
RESULTS FOR EACH STEP	Values we want to preserve and remember:	Key Issues that need to be addressed:	Vision Statement	Mission Statement:	SMART goals and objectives:	What we will have achieved by the end of next year two years from now three years from now

Refer to notes from the responses to questions at the end of chapter 4 (Reassess Our Current Ministry). Fill out the above chart with those responses regarding core values and key issues. Add more rows as needed for additional values, issues, etc. A template of this chart is available online.[2] Now you are ready to discern the vision God has for your church.

Vision

A vision statement should tell ourselves and others why the church exists. It is a statement about the nature of what it means to be church. A vision does not necessarily change with circumstances. A vision should remain constant for many years. Examples of clear and succinct church vision statements include:

- "Ginghamsburg Church . . . changing the world one life at a time."[3]

  The Ginghamsburg Church, Tipp City, Ohio

- "The vision of Ben Hill United Methodist Church is to equip and empower the body of Christ with a biblically based, global Christian ministry of love and concern through holistic care, prayer, evangelism, outreach, training, worship, and social consciousness to serve all God's people." The final sentence of their vision sums up everything: "We are a Christ-centered church where everybody is somebody."[4]

  Ben Hill United Methodist Church, Atlanta, Georgia

- "To transform lives, to transform our community and to renew the mainline church."[5]

  The United Methodist Church of the Resurrection, Leawood, Kansas

2. See the Ministry Action Plan template at https://www.dougruffle.com/roadmap-to-renewal-information/.

3. See http://ginghamsburg.org/bring/who-we-are/what-we-believe.

4. See http://benhillumc.org/our-vision-2/.

5. See http://www.cor.org/about-resurrection/beliefs-and-values/.

- "The purpose of The Story will be to inspire nonreligious Houstonians to play their part in the unfolding Story of God's love in Jesus Christ."[6]

St. Luke's United Methodist Church, Houston, Texas

Much attention has been given to vision statements. Too often such statements, once articulated, are forgotten or ignored. The purpose of drafting a concise and accurate vision statement is to bring clarity to the ministry of the church today and for the coming years. The prophet Micah articulated a vision for what God requires of us: to do justice, and to love kindness and to walk humbly with our God (Mic 6:8). God had done so much for the people; this vision articulates what God expects in return.

The question had been asked of God, "With what shall I come before the Lord, and bow myself before God on high?" (Mic 6:6). It is the age-old question of what we can do to please God. Micah's answer to the question shows that God is more interested in the way we live on a daily basis than by the rituals we offer.

The Westminster Shorter Catechism historically used by many Presbyterian and Reformed churches starts with the question, "What is the chief end of human beings?" The proper answer is, "To glorify God and enjoy him forever." This too is a question of purpose that goes to the heart of our existence. Vision statements have to do with our identity—who we *are*.

A clear and concise vision statement elicits an enthusiastic response on the part of members of the church and at the same time paints a vivid picture of the church for those outside of its membership. A vision statement helps the church gain clarity about where it is going and it helps those not yet part of the church to understand how the church envisions its future. Without a clear and concise vision statement, a church flutters around like a dry leaf on a blustery autumn day. The purpose and direction of the church become hard to grasp and the very identity of the church becomes ill-defined when we do not have a vision statement. If a church is to focus on the priorities of ministry and make

6. See http://www.stlukesmethodist.org/news_item?r=MACCFA6H74.

connections with its community, it needs a clear and concise vision statement that members will embrace and that gives direction to the work of church leaders.

Jesus preached and taught the vision of the reign of God breaking in to our earthly life. It was the central focus of ministry. His Sermon on the Mount lays out the vision. The Beatitudes (Matt 5:1–11) describe the characteristics of those who have decided to live in God's reign. They are the meek, the merciful, the pure in heart, the peacemakers. Together these reign of God subjects are the salt and light of the earth (Matt 5:13–15). They go beyond the letter of the law and live in the spirit of the law's deeper purpose for humanity. Their motivation for living by the rule of God comes not out of obligation to a law but rather from an internal attitude that understands relationships holistically. "So when you are offering your gift at the altar, if you remember that your brother or sister has something against you, leave your gift there before the altar and go; first be reconciled to your brother or sister, and then come and offer your gift" (Matt 5:22–24).

Jesus envisions living in a reign where relationships with fellow human beings are characterized by *agape* love—a love that seeks the well-being of the other. Agape love is based on God's self-sacrificing love for humanity. Chapter 5 of the Gospel of Matthew contains the characterization of the reign of God with Jesus' exhortation to "be perfect . . . as your heavenly Father is perfect" (Matt 5:48). By "perfect" Jesus does not mean *perfection* in life, as if it were possible not to make mistakes. He refers to balanced, holistic living infused with agape love for others. This is his vision for humanity. His preaching and teaching invite people to choose to live in this reign.

There is the paradox that the reign of God is both here and now and promises that something is yet to come. It is "here and now" for all those who choose to live in the spirit of Jesus' teaching. It does not come in its fullness until all humanity chooses to live by reign of God principles and reign of God agape love. The hope we have is that one day all will live in this reign that Jesus inaugurated with his presence on earth.

Vision is a powerful connection with God through prayerful discernment of what God is calling us to be and use of God-given imagination. One summer I followed the blog of my good friend Marcelle as she made the pilgrimage of St. James in France and Spain, a hike of more than one thousand miles across some rugged terrain, including the Pyrenees. She would comment on her journey on her blog. She commented on how often people would remark to her that they could not imagine making such an arduous journey.

Marcelle responded, "If I can imagine it, and can be open to the possibility, it is only a few steps before the possibility becomes reality. I have come to believe that imagination is our ability to be open to the dreams and possibilities God places in our heart. If I am open to the possibilities, God usually has a way of making the possibility a reality. I have learned not to place limitations on God by saying, 'I can't imagine doing . . .' because once I make that statement, I close myself to whatever dreams and possibilities God has for me."[7]

What an empowering statement of truth! If we can imagine, if we can be open to possibility, no telling what God will place in our hearts and what blessings we will experience along the way. This is an essential part of the task of creating a vision statement for the church. Discern and imagine.

Discern what God is calling you to be and imagine what you will look like when you have allowed God to complete the transformation. Picture what it will look like when you have reached your destination of realizing what God has called you to be.

The key question at this point in the road to renewal is: What is God calling us to *be* as a church? The response to this question is the beginning of a vision statement that is creative and imaginative. Such a statement should capture the essence of this calling. With clarity of vision, we can see where the road is taking us. We can envision what the destination place looks like. We still have

7. Reverend Marcelle Dotson's blog of her pilgrimage to Santiago de Campostela in "Camino 2007" can be found at http://camino-marcelle.blogspot.com/2008/08/safe-sound.html.

some miles to go before the journey of rediscovery is completed, but now we are confident that the road ahead will take us to a better place, a more God-infused, outward directed fulfillment of our mission.

Your Turn

As a group, spend some time responding to questions prompted by the vision of Micah and Jesus.

1. What does it mean to do justice in our community?

2. What does it mean today to love kindness in our community?

3. What would it look like for our church to walk humbly with our God?

4. What does it mean to choose to live in God's reign today?

At this point in the road to renewal, invite a group of two or three persons from your team to work on the creation of a vision statement. Have others in the team covenant to pray for them in this task. The writing team will take into consideration all that has been learned so far in the journey. They will prepare a concise statement that they bring to the larger team for review and reshaping at the next meeting. The team charged with this task is invited to use the following questions to guide their crafting of the vision statement. Others on the team are invited to spend time during their daily devotional to pray about and reflect on these same questions (and to share insights with the "Vision Team"):

1. Considering what we have discerned and discovered so far in this journey, for what and/or for whom does our church exist?

2. Nonreligious people are those who do not profess faith in any religious system nor do they participate in a community of faith. Nominally religious people are those who profess belief in a religious system in name only. That is, they say they belong to a particular religious faith, but their actions reflect

87

nonparticipation. The question for our church is: Why will the nonreligious and nominally religious people in our area discover the blessing of forming part of our community of faith?

3. Try to put into a sentence the essence of the responses made to questions 1 and 2 above.

As you wrestle with the above questions, consider gathering focus groups of members and attenders of the church to ask these same questions. In this way, you will be gaining important input from those beyond the leadership team.

8

Realign Mission, Goals, and Objectives

THE FAMILIAR PASSAGE OF the Great Commission from the Gospel of Matthew (28:16–20) has been the clarion call for mission for years. The danger of familiarity with that statement is that we sometimes become blind to new insights and meanings. I invite you to read the passage from the perspective of the mission statement your team will create.

Jesus painted a picture of a preferred future for humankind by teaching and preaching the reign of God. The reign was the vision; the Great Commission was the mission. The reign of God is all about what we are called to *be* while the Great Commission is all about what we are called to *do*.

Remember the context of commission in the Gospel of Matthew. The passage begins, "Now the eleven disciples went to Galilee." It is significant that Matthew mentions eleven. Previously Matthew mentions "the twelve" as the life of Jesus was narrated. It became almost a pat phrase. "Then Jesus summoned his twelve disciples and gave them authority . . ." (10:1); "These twelve Jesus sent out with the following instructions . . ." (10:5); "Now when Jesus had finished instructing his twelve disciples . . ." (11:1); "While Jesus was going up to Jerusalem, he took the twelve disciples aside by themselves, and said to them . . ." (20:17). There were always twelve. Even if we understand "the Twelve" as a symbolic term, a later interpretation of the church read back into Jesus' day, the mention of "eleven" here still evokes attention. The full contingent of followers is diminished. Where there were always twelve, now there are eleven.[1]

The specter of Judas is present as his absence is noted. Here we have a group in decline. They've gone from twelve to eleven. Before the church was even the church, it was experiencing decline. These were not bold witnesses for Jesus Christ. And yet Jesus showed faith in these followers. He gave them a commission. The disciples were not an army of believers ready for battle. They were a struggling community as much in need of being evangelized as a group ready for the ministry of evangelizing others. The passage comes at the very end of the gospel of Matthew. The story has been told of Jesus: his birth, his life and ministry, his passion, death, and resurrection. This is the final scene. The resurrected Jesus meets for a final time with his disciples at the appointed place in Galilee. Jesus is about to return to the Father.

The followers went to Galilee, "to the mountain to which Jesus had directed them" (Matt 28:16b). There are twelve other references in Matthew's gospel to mountains or mounts. More than a geographical location, "mountain" in Matthew is a place where revelation occurs. He gave his most famous sermon "on the Mount." He was transfigured on a mountain. He would go off to pray on a mountain. The followers of Jesus have gone to a mountain. Matthew is also informing us, the readers, of the fact that we are about to share in a revelation experience—where God's word will be spoken and God's purpose unveiled for the followers.

Verse 17 about the disciples is most revealing. When they saw Jesus, they worshiped him, but some doubted. This is not a triumphant army ready for battle. Doubt exists. Not everyone is convicted and convinced. The same could be said for today. Traditional Protestant churches decline in influence and membership has left these denominations struggling with questions of identity.

---

1. Form critics see "the Twelve" as a later addition to Scripture. See Bultmann, *History of the Synoptic Tradition*, 345.

Internal political turmoil manifests a lack of consensus regarding a common vision.

The final scene of Matthew presents worshipers and doubters together. There is great irony in this passage. Jesus the Christ has been given all authority in heaven and earth to commission his followers to go into the world making disciples and baptizing them. He gives that commission to a group of people diminished in number and pervaded by doubt. To these followers who had abandoned him in his most difficult moment, he calls to teach nations and observe all that he had commanded. Where will the strength come to respond to such a commission?

Jesus left his followers with a promise: "And remember, I am with you always, to the end of the age." Followers seeking to fulfill the commission do not go alone. The resurrected Lord promises to go along, "for I am with you." There are lessons that can be drawn for churches embarking on the road to renewal. Despite a possible downturn of membership, now is not the time to despair. The gospel message urges us to move forward and to continue to articulate a vision of faith. It also tells us to be about the business of carrying the message of the gospel to others.

There is a tendency to hold back when lack of consensus or doubt is present. There is a tendency to think that we should get our own house in order before attempting to go to others with a message. Yet Jesus commanded worshipers and doubters to "go therefore and make disciples of all nations" (Matt 28:19a). Jesus had faith that followers would share the good news filled with the Holy Spirit.

Juan Damián, a Methodist minister from Uruguay once served as Director of the Latin American Schools of Evangelization (ELADE) for the Council of Evangelical Methodist Churches in Latin America and the Caribbean, repeats the mantra, "We evangelize ourselves while evangelizing."[2] Transformation happens to those of us engaged in evangelization when we engage in its ministry.

2. See Damián, *Carta de Evangelización*, and Damián, *Unidos*. Translation by Douglas Ruffle.

Writing a Mission Statement (What Are We Called to Do?)

The reign of God, then, is the vision. The Great Commission is the mission. We hold these two in a macro picture of what the church is called to be and do. Local churches need to bring the macro to the micro. Local churches are called to articulate the vision God has called them to be and the mission God has called them to do for a specific context and time.

Mission statements address key issues that the church faces and, in light of the vision it has for ministry and its core values, articulates what it will do. It answers the question, "Given our current situation and context, what is God calling our church to do?" It serves as the driving force for your MAP. Sometimes churches call these "purpose statements." The point is to draft a concise sentence that tells people, both insiders to the church and outsiders, what your church does.

Some samples of mission statements include:

- The United Methodist Church of the Resurrection, Leawood, Kansas, refers to their statement as their purpose: "To build a Christian community where non-religious and nominally religious people are becoming deeply committed Christians."[3]

- The Ginghamsburg Church in Tipp City, Ohio, articulated their mission around three key words: *celebration, cell,* and *call.* Their mission statement reads:

  ° *Bring seeking people into a life-CELEBRATION with Jesus*

  ° *Grow as disciples in CELL community*

  ° *Serve out of our CALL and giftedness*[4]

---

3. http://www.cor.org/campus/leawood (reference the sidebar on "About Resurrection").

4. http://ginghamsburg.org/bring/who-we-are/what-we-believe.

- Washington Crossing United Methodist Church articulates their mission as "empowering people to become totally devoted disciples of Jesus Christ in mission to the world."[5]

You could preface each of these statements by saying, "What is our church called to do? "We are called to . . ." and you complete the sentence. An important addition to the formula for writing a mission statement is two words: "so that . . ." It answers the question, "Why are we called to do this mission?"

A church in an urban area of metropolitan New York concluded that its mission was to minister to single parents. This is what they were called *to do*. The church discovered, however, that identifying its niche, its focus for mission, was not enough. Why minister to single parents? What is the overarching goal of this mission ministry? What will happen to these single parents as a result of the mission of the church?

The Church of the Resurrection answers that in the second half of its purpose statement: "are becoming deeply committed Christians." Their mission is to reach nonreligious and nominally religious persons *so that* they become deeply committed Christians. It is not enough to offer a service to the people as part of the mission. We are called by God to become instruments of transformation that can occur with them. The urban church focuses on single parents *so that* these single parents can become deeply committed to the life-saving reign of God principles of Jesus Christ.

Once the leadership team has gained clarity about its mission, it assigns several members to craft the mission statement. To follow the analogy of the road trip, two or three of the travelers are dropped off at a park while the others find a place to stay for the night. The two or three gather notes from the journey and work on the wording of a statement that accurately reflects the destination God is leading them to. The mission statement will describe succinctly what the church is called to do so that . . .

Once crafted, the two or three wordsmiths rejoin the leadership team to perfect it. Good mission statements should be

---

5. http://www.crossingumc.org/about-us/we-believe/.

able to be printed on the back of a T-shirt. The more succinct it is, the greater possibility that people will grasp the power of the mission laid before them. It should be a statement that is easily remembered.

Here are some sample mission statements from the world of business:[6]

- Walt Disney: "To make people happy."

- Merck: "To preserve and improve human life."

- Wal-Mart: "To give ordinary folk the chance to buy the same things as rich people."

These are succinct statements that capture the heart of the company's mission. In these business examples, perhaps the "so that" is understood and therefore not mentioned. Each of these businesses desires to make a profit. Similarly, some church mission statements leave off the "so that" part because it may seem obvious to them.

Here are some sample mission statements from churches that do not articulate the "so that" clause:

- To connect people to Jesus Christ and to each other.

- Proclaiming the gospel of Jesus Christ to those who have never heard and stirring churches to greater evangelistic and missions outreach.

- Building disciples; Growing in faith; Serving in Christ's name.

- To allow God to work in us, with us, through us, and for us in the accomplishment of his purpose.

- To know Jesus Christ, to serve him in joyful obedience and to make him known by growing disciples, planting churches and renewing communities.

- A Spirit-filled Community Actively Leading People to Christ and Christ-likeness.

6. See http://www.family-business-experts.com/sample-mission-statements.html.

- Trinity Church is a fellowship seeking to share the love and word of Jesus Christ with all.

These are fine statements. However, they would be even better if they included a phrase that explained why they do what they do.

Here are a few samples from churches that have included the "so that" portion:

- University United Methodist Church in San Antonio, Texas, draws from their denominational statement: "To help people look to Jesus and live like Jesus in order to make disciples of Jesus Christ for the transformation of the world."[7] They provide the secondary clause that tells us the "why" of what they do.

- Urban Village, a multi-campus church in Chicago, Illinois, that started in 2009, articulates their beliefs, values, core practices and strategies, all of which help give clarity to their catch line to be "Bold, Inclusive, and Relevant." Their strategies articulate why they do what they do: "God is calling Urban Village Church to create Jesus-loving, inclusive communities that ignite the city." Always pay attention to what comes after the word "that" in a mission or strategy statement. It helps complete the thought and gives a more well-rounded picture of what the church is all about.[8]

- Cornerstone Church is a United Methodist multi-campus ministry in the Grand Rapids, Michigan, area. Their succinct mission statement gives the "so that" when they articulate: "Helping people know Jesus and make him known." To proclaim the gospel, transform lives and make disciples for Jesus Christ.[9]

- First United Methodist Church in San Diego, California, includes succinct statements of their mission, vision, and also a "statement of inclusivity" in the "About" section of their

7. http://www.theu.org/what-we-believe/.
8. http://www.urbanvillagechurch.org/beliefs/.
9. http://www.cornerstonemi.org/im-new/about-us.

website. Their mission is adopted from the denomination's statement: "To make disciples of Jesus Christ for the transformation of the world." The United Methodist Church first made that statement at their 1996 General Conference. At the time it simply stated, "To make disciples of Jesus Christ." At a subsequent General Conference, the phrase "for the transformation of the world" was added. The latter phrase gives the "so that" completion to the mission. It is as if they are saying, "Make disciples *so that* the world can be transformed." First San Diego's statement of inclusivity "affirms that all individuals are of sacred worth without exception. All means all."[10] It makes a statement to the community that everyone has a place in their community of faith.

Each of these statements includes an explanation sentence or phrases that tells us the why of the mission. Urban Village wants to ignite the city of Chicago through the communities of faith formed. Cornerstone's simple statement explains that they want their people to help make Jesus known in their city. San Diego First's statement includes an additional word about what they mean regarding inclusivity. These expressions of belief and these mission statements help the churches themselves know what they are all about. The statements also serve the community to inform people about the character and values of their particular expression of the church.

Your mission statement should be a reflection of what your church *does*. For the purpose of greater clarity I would encourage a church to include the "so that" kind of clause that tells more about the "why you do what you do." Both church insiders and those outside will understand more clearly the purpose of the mission. Once the leadership team has had an opportunity to refine the statement, then it is time to bring it before the governing body of the church for further perfection and ratification.

10. http://www.fumcsd.org/about/mission-statement/.

Goals, Objectives, and a Timeline

Goals and objectives flow out of the mission statement and give specificity to what the church plans to accomplish. Begin the task of defining goals and objectives by narrowing what three to five activities the church will do to accomplish its mission. Goals should be SMART, which is an acronym for "Specific, Measurable, Achievable, Relevant to the mission, and carried out within a Timeframe."

Hilltop United Methodist Church in Sandy, Utah, dedicated a large part of a monthly newsletter to explain what a SMART goal is and how it helps their church find clarity of mission. They were encouraging the leaders of the church to articulate SMART goals for the areas of responsibility they each had. The mission statement for Hilltop also includes a "so that" clause: "Hilltop—a place to belong, believe and become so that God's Reign can come, so that God's will be done."[11]

Christ Church United Methodist, in Chattanooga, Tennessee, articulated SMART goals for their Ministry Plan.[12] The plan points to the church's strengths, challenges, threats and opportunities. They also underscored their core values. They assessed community needs that they felt they could serve. Their plan articulates what vital congregations need to emphasize, namely, a church that has disciples who worship, who make new disciples, who grow in their faith, who get involved in mission, and who give to mission. Their plan is an excellent example of employing a discernment and discovery process to come up with SMART goals.

As you develop your goals and objectives, make sure to align people with projects. If the goal or objective is stated as a church goal, but no one is assigned the responsibility to complete it, chances are it won't get done. Put the goal and objective in writing and assign the person or team that will be responsible for achieving it. Answer the question, "Who will do what by when?"

11. See http://www.hilltopumchurch.org/docs/Newsletters/October%20 2013.pdf and the website for Hilltop UMC: www.hilltopumchurch.org.

12. See http://christchurchchatt.org/pdfs/CallToAction.pdf.

Use the following chart for the goals and objectives of your MAP.

Goal	Objective	Who will do?	By When?

Gaining clarity about your church's mission, goals and objectives will set the course of ministry for the next chapter in the history of your church. You need a target to hit a bull's-eye. Mission statements, goals and objectives give you specifics to aim at.

Your Turn

Read Matthew 28:16–20 out loud and slowly. Respond to the following questions.

1. What is the significance that there were "eleven" disciples?

2. What words or phrases of this passage leap off the page to speak to you?

3. What does this passage have to do with defining the mission for your church today?

4. What is this passage calling your church to do?

5. Assign a team of people to draft a mission statement for the church and bring it to the next meeting of the leadership team for refinement.

9

Roadmarkers on the Road to Renewal

AS YOU PIECE TOGETHER the work you have done on the road to renewal, you have all of the elements for your Ministry Action Plan (MAP). You have clarified core values, articulated vision and mission statements and established goals and objectives. Now you need to place roadmarkers for your way ahead. A roadmark is how you evaluate the effectiveness of your MAP so that you can monitor its progress and make any needed adjustments. Your leadership team has engaged in a journey of rediscovery and now it wants to make sure that the implementation of the plan goes smoothly.

Roadmarkers are set along our roadmap to keep us on track to reach our destination. If we want to travel the road from Asbury Park, New Jersey, to Chicago, Illinois, we place a mark on the map to indicate that we had better reach Cleveland by the end of the first day if we are to reach our destination in time. Similarly, we set roadmarkers on the journey ahead of us as we seek to implement the elements of our MAP. For instance, if we have set a measurable goal of increasing worship attendance by 25 percent within a two-year period, what will be the roadmarkers that we can set at six months, nine months, and a year? If, after a year, we have not increased our attendance by 5 percent, what adjustments must we make in order to reach the goal? Roadmarkers help keep us on track.

The essence of roadmarkers for the road to renewal is that we have in place a timeline for the implementation of our Ministry Action Plan. In the timeline we can look to specific dates when we can measure progress toward the fulfillment of goals. There are four key questions we need to answer now that we have devised the MAP. (1) How do we get the entire church out on the road to reach the destination? (2) What resources will we need along the way? (3) Who will be driving? (4) How will we know we have reached our destination?

How Do We Get the Entire Church Out on the Road to Reach the Destination?

The congregation must take ownership of the road to renewal if ever they have a chance of arriving at that preferred destination. When the leadership team communicates frequently with the larger community of faith there is a greater chance for them to embrace the vision of the road ahead. This can be accomplished through frequent use of "mission moments" during worship when members of the team can share about their journey and the lessons learned. Here the pastor plays a key role in keeping the congregation informed.

Once the MAP is in place, the pastor needs to keep it before the congregation through sermons, newsletters, reminders at meetings, and other opportunities. One of the reasons that the United Methodist Church of the Resurrection has moved forward in growth and vitality is that the pastor, Adam Hamilton, continually keeps the vision of the church before people. He manages to remind people of the mission of the church ("To build a Christian community where nonreligious and nominally religious people are becoming deeply committed Christians") in almost every sermon. The Reverend Brian Eble, while serving as pastor of the First United Methodist Church in Oakhurst, New Jersey, led the congregation in reciting their mission statement as part of the liturgy each time they worshipped.

There are other ways to keep the vision and mission of the church before the people so that they can embrace them. One church posts its vision statement on the inside door of the bathroom stalls! Other churches have put them on mugs for the congregation to give out to church visitors. Another church hangs a banner in their worship center keeping the mission of the church constantly before the eyes of the people. The idea is to help people get on board—to help them incorporate the vision and mission of the church into their own hearts and minds so that the church can go on their journey of mission and ministry together.

What Resources Do We Need along the Way?

A complete MAP considers the costs of implementation—both financial and human. How much do we need to budget to help make our goals and objectives a reality? How many people need to be involved? What training do they need? Who will do the training? How much will it cost?

Jesus spoke of the importance of calculating costs. He used the analogy of a builder who must first take stock of his resources before embarking on his project. "For which of you, intending to build a tower, does not first sit down and estimate the cost to see whether he has enough to complete it?" (Luke 14:28). Jesus was talking about the cost of discipleship. Indeed, careful planning for the mission and ministry of the church is part of the cost of what it means to be a disciple. As we review the MAP we need to take stock of the resources we have to go forward.

Who Will Be Driving?

The successful implementation of your MAP requires the assignment of persons or teams to each goal and objective. Someone needs to be assigned to monitor the charts on pages 83 and 99 so that there is an accountability system in place for implementation. The "monitor" keeps track of the larger picture of the implementation of the plan. He or she oversees the progress of each part of the plan so that roadmarks are met in a timely manner. At the implementation stage, the navigator assumes the role of monitor. Now that we have a MAP, the monitor makes sure we stay on course.

The monitor also gauges how well the church is accomplishing goals and objectives by their appointed end dates. He or she asks, "Have we accomplished what our MAP says we should have accomplished?" The monitor gives updates at each meeting of the church's governing board and indicates when goals and objectives have been reached or if they have not been reached. Celebrate the victories along the way. If you have come close to meeting the roadmarkers, throw a party!

If the monitor sees that a goal or objective has not been met, she brings this to the attention of the governing body of the church or the leadership team that worked on the roadmap. Find out why the roadmark was not reached. Make adjustments to the plan so that you have a better chance of being successful.

How Will We Know When We Have Reached Our Destination?

The overarching goal for the roadmap to renewal is for the local church to rediscover its mission. You know you will have reached your destination when the church has gained clarity around its mission and has an action plan in place to fulfill it. We said at the beginning that the entire process needs to be infused with prayer. The roadmap to renewal has been all about waiting on God and discerning what God wants us to be and do in this moment in the life of our church. We remember the words of the prophet Isaiah when he wrote, "But those who wait for the Lord shall renew their strength, they shall mount up with wings like eagles, they shall run and not be weary, they shall walk and not faint" (Isa 40:31).

We engage this road precisely to renew our strength as a congregation and to gain the confidence and endurance to go forth in mission and ministry with vitality. While you have measurable goals that will indicate whether or not you have met the roadmarkers of the MAP, there is a greater sense of movement when the congregation is clear about its mission. This clarity of purpose and vision will infuse hope for the future.

One of my favorite contemporary songs, "Shout to the Lord," includes the line "Nothing compares to the promise I have in you." The promise of Jeremiah gives joy for those who travel the road to renewal. God has plan for us, plans to give us a future with hope (cf. Jer 29:11).

Now That We Have Arrived, What's Next?

The goal of the roadmap to renewal is to rediscover the mission of the church. The destination is a place where the church has articulated clear vision and mission statements and put together a Ministry Action Plan (MAP) that will provide a roadmap for the next stage in the life and history of the church.

Change happens frequently in our world. Your roadmap should be reviewed after two or three years of its implementation. Make any needed adjustments to your original plan during those first two to three years. Before your church becomes complacent, take another road trip to rediscover once again what God is calling your church to be and do.

Your Turn

1. As a leadership team, determine the intermediate roadmarks you will use to monitor the success of your Ministry Action Plan (MAP).

2. What are the financial and human resources you will need to carry out your MAP?

3. Who will be assigned to serve as the MAP's monitor and how will he or she communicate progress to the larger congregation?

Home

I remember as a child the comfort of hearing my mom and dad sing the line from the old nursery rhyme, "home again, home again, jiggity jig," as we pulled onto our street after being away. No matter how long or short the trip, coming home felt good.

There should be comfort and celebration upon arriving home from the road trip to renewal. We should be able to see home in a new light. A quiet confidence infuses the familiar surroundings. The discoveries made on the road bring new meaning and purpose to the mission and ministry we have.

Lest we forget the lessons learned on the road, we need to remind ourselves of our new MAP as we continue the work of the local church. We should not allow the comfort of home to lull us into old habits and go about the "same old same old." We now have a strategy, a plan to move ourselves forward so that we can fulfill the promise that God has for our congregation, a promise to give us a future with hope.

During the implementation of our action plan, we need to review and evaluate it continually. "Are we doing what we set out to do?" "Are we reaching our goals?" "Do we need to make any adjustments?"

God gives to each congregation the resources its needs to fulfill its purpose. The life of prayer that supported our road trip continues to keep us connected to God and to one another as we minister from home. A good MAP should lead the way for at least several years. However, whenever we feel like we have somehow lost vision for the reason for our existence or lost traction for what we are called to do, we know we can get back into our vehicles to take another road trip to rediscover all over again what God has called us to.

May your journey be blessed and bring much fruit for the sake of the reign of God.

Study Guide

Roadmap to Renewal is an invitation to rediscover what God is calling a church to be and do. The questions in the "Your Turn" section at the end of each chapter are designed to help guide a team of people from the local church through a process of both discovery and rediscovery. In their journey of discovery, participants will uncover who they are and who lives in the surrounding community. In their journey of rediscovery, they will uncover a fresh vision for the mission to which God invites them.

This study guide is designed to be a resource for the leadership team as they work their way through this process. There are ten sessions that correspond directly to the *Roadmap to Renewal* book, beginning with the introduction. When, how long, and how often the team will meet will need to be decided upon by the team itself.

It is our prayer that, through this process, the leadership team will be drawn more closely together and will become the leaven that will help the whole church become more outwardly oriented—a true missional church.

In the appendix of this guide, there are supplemental resources, including a sample announcement to the congregation during worship and a liturgy to consecrate members of the team. There is also a sample survey to solicit input from the congregation as a whole. If the survey is used, gather this information early on in the process.

Introduction: Readiness

Choosing a GPS (Guided Process Servant)

Talk to your conference staff person responsible for congregational development about possible "Guided Process Servants" or coaches who could accompany a leadership team from your church. The Guided Process Servant should be able to ask good questions, be a good listener and be able to follow the process as outlined in the book *Roadmap to Renewal: Rediscovering the Church's Mission*.

Planning the Road Trip

Objective: By the end of this session, participants will have gained an understanding of the process involved for engaging the *Roadmap to Renewal* and will have begun to build themselves into a leadership team.

Assignment prior to the session: Read the "Welcome" and "Introduction: Readiness" sections of the book (pp. 1–15).

Agenda for the meeting:

OPENING PRAYER

INTRODUCTIONS

Engage in an exercise to get to know one another better. Pair up with another member of the team and share with each other information about: (a) your hometown; (b) how you came to be part of this church; and (c) one bit of information that people may not know about you. When ample time has passed for sharing, have the partners introduce each other to the larger group.

SCRIPTURE READING: LUKE 24:13–35

DISCUSSION

1. Assign someone to take notes on behalf of the group.

2. Read the "Welcome" section on p. 7 as a group. Invite discussion about the process outlined in *Roadmap to Renewal.* As a group, respond to the question, "What expectations do you have for this roadtrip?"

3. Respond to the questions in the "Your Turn" section at the end of the introduction.

4. Determine if the leadership team will be consecrated for the task during a worship service. (For a sample liturgy for such a consecration, see the appendix.)

CLOSING PRAYER

Looking to the next session: Read chapter 1, "Reality Check." Jot down thoughts and responses to the questions in the "Your Turn" section at the end of the chapter to be shared with the team.

Chapter 1: Reality Check

Reading the Signs

Objective: By the end of this session, participants will have gained insight as to how their congregation measures according to an ecumenical consensus of the understanding of what it means to be a church serving as a "sign, preview, and instrument" of the reign of God.

Assignment prior to the session: Read chapter 1, "Reality Check."

(To gain more information and input from a wider group, consider surveying the congregation. The appendix to this study guide includes a sample survey. If used, assign members of the leadership team to collect the information and report at this session.)

Agenda for the meeting:

OPENING PRAYER

PREPARING TO CONNECT WITH THE COMMUNITY

In anticipation of the "driving around" portion of the roadmap process, begin to discuss the people you will be contacting as part of the exercise to learn about community perceptions of your congregation. How will you engage in "ministry by walking around?" Which town leaders will you contact? Who will do the contacting? When will you "drive around" to see your community with fresh eyes? Assign someone from the group to collect demographic data.

SCRIPTURE READING: MATT 6:25–34

DISCUSSION

1. Make sure someone takes notes and keeps them together with other notes from the roadtrip.

2. Respond to questions 1 through 6 in the "Your Turn" section at the end of chapter 1.

3. Discuss the statement, "The mission-oriented church rediscovers the needs of its surrounding community and world and engages in ministry to address those needs."

4. Using a flip chart, write down responses to question 7, "What are the items that your 'scorecard' uses to measure church effectiveness?"

5. Report findings from the congregational survey, if used.

CLOSING PRAYER

Looking to the next session: Read chapter 2, "Reconnect." Jot down thoughts and responses to the questions in the "Your Turn" section at the end of the chapter to be shared with the team.

Chapter 2: Reconnect

Avoiding Roadkill

Objective: By the end of this session, participants will have worked on the prayer foundation for the roadmap process.

Assignment prior to the session: Read chapter 2 "Reconnect."

Agenda for the meeting:

OPENING PRAYER

THE CENTRALITY OF PRAYER

Prayer needs to undergird any process of renewal in the life of a church. Discuss together the meaning of prayer and prayer practices in the life of participants of the group. Consider teaming up with another person from the leadership team to form "prayer partners" where you will check in with each other at least once a week to pray either in person or by telephone.

SCRIPTURE READING: Ps 34:1–10

DISCUSSION

1. Make sure someone takes notes and keeps them together with other notes from the roadtrip.

2. Respond to the questions in the "Your Turn" section at the end of chapter 2.

3. Review plans for "ministry by walking around" (MBWA), "driving around" and "town leader" interviews. In the previous session, team members were invited to plan ahead for the exercise of MBWA, driving around together and arranging

interviews with town leaders. Report back to one another on progress for these plans.

Looking to the next session: Read chapter 3, "Rediscover the Landscape of Our Parish." Jot down thoughts and responses to the questions in the "Your Turn" section at the end of the chapter to be shared with the team.

Go out with another team member or members to engage in ministry by walking around. The questions on p. 46 will help you gather information. Think of some of your own questions to ask people, as well.

Make arrangements to drive around your parish before the next session. Plan to get out of the vehicle from time to time to ask questions and take notes about what you see. Arrange to visit town leaders following the suggested questions on p. 46.

Chapter 3: Rediscover the Landscape of Our Parish

Driving Around

Objective: By the end of the session, the leadership team will have collected pertinent information regarding the characteristics of the parish your church serves. This information will serve as a building block for putting together a Ministry Action Plan (MAP) as the roadmap process continues moving forward.

Assignment prior to session: Read chapter 3, "Rediscover the Landscape of Our Parish." Collect demographic information about your parish area and have someone make printouts of this information for everyone on the team. Engage in activities that take you outside your church walls via "driving around," "MBWA," and interviews with key leaders in the community.

(As a way to gather information from influential leaders in the town, in addition to the personal interviews, one church hosted a "panel discussion" inviting an owner of a real estate office, the president of a community organization (i.e., Kiwanis, Rotary), a member of the town council, and a guidance counselor from the public school. The leadership team engaged in conversation with the panel about the needs of the community and the community's perception of their church.)

Agenda for the meeting:

OPENING PRAYER

DEMOGRAPHICS

Distribute copies of demographic data obtained from the US Census Bureau or from your judicatory's subscription service. Appoint someone from the team to give interpretation of the data, including population trends and how ethnic diversity is or is not changing the landscape of your parish area. Discuss surprising or new information.

SCRIPTURE READING: 1 COR 9:20–23

DISCUSSION

1. Make sure someone takes notes and keeps them together with other notes from the road trip.

2. Respond to the questions in the "Your Turn" section at the end of chapter 3.

3. Discuss together what it might mean in your parish to "become all things to all people," for the sake of the gospel.

CLOSING PRAYER

Looking to the next session: Read chapter 4, "Reassess Our Current Ministry," and jot down thoughts and responses to the questions in the "Your Turn" section at the end of the chapter to be shared with the team.

Chapter Four: Reassess Our Current Ministry

Rechecking the Map

Objective: By the end of the session, the leadership team will have honestly assessed the current ministry of the church, identified key issues it needs to address, and identified core values.

Assignment prior to session: Read chapter 4, "Reassess Our Current Ministry."

Agenda for the meeting:

OPENING PRAYER

CORE VALUES

Core values of a church help define its theology of mission engagement. When it comes time to articulate vision and mission, core values provide a reference point. Take time to discuss the core values of the United Methodist Church.

SCRIPTURE READING: PROV 11:13; 2 COR 12:19–20

DISCUSSION

1. Make sure someone takes notes and keeps them together with other notes from the road trip.

2. Discuss together what it means to be "built up" as a community of faith, especially in light of the litany of things the Apostle Paul would fear to find as recorded in the passage from 2 Corinthians.

3. Respond to the questions in the "Your Turn" section at the end of the chapter. As you share responses in the context of the entire team, seek consensus around the most important issues identified.

4. Prioritize what should be continued, stopped, and started, and then focus on three to five key issues the church faces as it discerns God's guidance into the future.

5. Assign one or two members of the team to research the issues that you identified. When taking the upcoming "road break," visit another church; see if the visited church has dealt with similar issues and ask how they handled them. Call a judicatory leader for suggestions of churches or pastors who have dealt with similar issues. Prepare to report findings at the next session.

CLOSING PRAYER

Looking to the next session: Read chapter 5, "Road Break," and jot down thoughts and responses to the questions in the "Your Turn" section at the end of the chapter to be shared with the team.

Chapter Five: Road Break

Rest Stops and Welcome Centers

Objective: By the end of the session, the leadership team will have debriefed from a visit to a teaching church and will have discussed together the meaning and importance of hospitality.

Assignment prior to the session: Read chapter 5, "Road Break." Make a "road break" visit to another church; see if the visited church dealt with similar issues and ask how they handled them.

Agenda for the meeting:

OPENING PRAYER

SCRIPTURE READING: HEB 13:1–2

Discuss together this passage and how it translates into modern-day hospitality in the church.

DISCUSSION

1. Make sure someone takes notes and keeps them together with other notes from the road trip.

2. Respond to questions 1 through 4 in the "Your Turn" section at the end of the chapter.

3. Give time to the one or two team members who have researched issues (question 4) and discuss together their findings.

4. Using a flip chart, in response to question 5, list core values that the church holds dear. Discuss.

5. Using the list of core values, have the group formulate ground rules for leadership team behavior as they move on "down the road."

CLOSING PRAYER

Looking to the next session: Read chapter 6, "Reaching Younger People," and jot down thoughts and responses to the questions in the "Your Turn" section at the end of the chapter to be shared with the team.

Chapter Six: Reaching Younger People

Opening the Doors

Objective: By the end of the session, the leadership team will have discussed together how to begin conversations with younger adults about faith in Christ and the church.

Assignment prior to the session: Read chapter 6, "Reaching Younger People," and jot down notes in response to the questions in the "Your Turn" section at the end of the chapter.

Agenda for the meeting:

OPENING PRAYER

SCRIPTURE READING: GAL 2:11–14

DISCUSSION

1. Make sure someone takes notes and keeps them together with other notes from the road trip.

2. How does this passage from Galatians help inform us about reaching new and different cultures with the gospel of Jesus Christ?

3. Spend the majority of your time together discussing questions 1 through 3 in the "Your Turn" section at the end of the chapter.

4. In response to question 4, discuss the term "missionary mindset" and how this mindset will help cross the culture divide to reach younger adults.

5. Develop some "action steps" in response to questions 3 and 4 and write them on a flip chart. Determine how you will follow up on the implementation of those steps.

CLOSING PRAYER

Looking to the next session: Read chapter 7, "Roadmaps Start with Vision," and jot down thoughts and responses to the questions in the "Your Turn" section at the end of the chapter to be shared with the team.

Chapter 7: Roadmaps Start with Vision

Choosing a Destination

Objective: By the end of the session, the leadership team will have gained clarity about the content of a Ministry Action Plan (MAP) and will have begun to articulate a vision statement for the church.

Assignment prior to the session: Read chapter 7, "Roadmaps Start with Vision."

Agenda for the meeting:

OPENING PRAYER

VISION

Vision is a powerful connection with God. It offers prayerful discernment of what God is calling us to be and shows us how to use of our God-given imagination. A vision statement helps the church gain clarity about where it is going.

SCRIPTURE READING: MIC 6:6–8

DISCUSSION

1. Make sure someone takes notes and keeps them together with other notes from the road trip.

2. Spend time responding to questions prompted by the vision of Micah (the same questions which are in the "Your Turn" section at the end of the chapter).

3. Begin working on your Vision. Invite a general discussion on visioning from the entire group. What important information does the group want to convey to the Vision Statement Team as they begin work on a statement?

4. Designate a "Vision Statement Team" to work on the articulation of a vision that reflects the work done so far.

CLOSING PRAYER

Looking to the next session: Read chapter 8, "Realign Mission, Goals, and Objectives," and jot down thoughts and responses to the questions in the "Your Turn" section at the end of the chapter to be shared with the team.

Chapter 8: Realign Mission, Goals, and Objectives

Resetting the Course

Objective: By the end of the session, the leadership team will have begun to articulate a mission statement for the church and will have begun to fill in the ingredients for a complete Ministry Action Plan.

Assignment prior to the session: Read chapter 8, "Realign Mission, Goals, and Objectives."

Agenda for the meeting:

OPENING PRAYER

SCRIPTURE READING: MATT 28:16-20

DISCUSSION

1. Make sure someone takes notes and keeps them together with other notes from the road trip.

2. Respond to questions in the "Your Turn" section at the end of the chapter.

3. Discuss with the team what they feel God is calling them to do from what they have learned on this journey so far.

4. Using the chart on p. 99, discuss the goals and objectives of a Ministry Action Plan.

5. Begin work on a Mission Statement. Assign two or three persons from the leadership team to draft a Mission Statement to be discussed at the next meeting. Before sending them out on their task, discuss together the elements the entire group wishes to remember.

CLOSING PRAYER

Looking to the next session: Read chapter 9, "Roadmarkers on the Road to Renewal," and jot down thoughts and responses to the questions in the "Your Turn" section at the end of the chapter to be shared with the team. Read the epilogue of the book. Assign two or three persons to work on filling in the chart included in chapter 7 (p. 83). As a team, schedule a time when you will present your Ministry Action Plan, including vision and mission statements, to the governing board of your church.

Chapter 9: Roadmarkers on the Road to Renewal

Reaching Your Destination

Objective: By the end of the session, the leadership team will have delineated the benchmarks or "roadmarkers" for the Ministry Action Plan.

Assignment prior to the session: Read chapter 9, "Roadmarkers on the Road to Renewal," and the epilogue of the book.

Agenda for the meeting:

OPENING PRAYER

SCRIPTURE READING: JER 29:10–14 AND JER 31:21

Jeremiah wrote letters to the people of Israel living in exile in Babylon assuring them of God's plans for them. In ch. 31, Jeremiah addresses the Israelites who were on their way to exile, exhorting them to place roadmarkers on their way so that they would be able to find their way back home. In light of all that your team has learned together, and the plans you have discerned that God has given, begin to articulate the roadmarkers by which you will find your way home to a place where ministry is vital and you are fulfilling the promise God has for you.

DISCUSSION

1. Make sure someone takes notes and keeps them together with other notes from the road trip.

2. Discuss the questions found in the "Your Turn" section at the end of the chapter.

3. Review plans for presenting your MAP to the governing board of the church.

4. Evaluate the journey you have just completed. How has it helped? What would have made the journey better?

5. Please send your comments and suggestions, including ways to improve this study guide, to: Druffle@gmail.com.

CLOSING PRAYER

Supplemental Resources for *Roadmap to Renewal*

Sample Announcement to the Congregation about the Roadmap Process during a Worship Service

Good morning:

Over the past two years, the Administrative Council—which, as you know, is comprised of the heads of the various ministry teams of the church—has attended two retreats with the objective of assessing who we at [your church name] are and where we want to go as a congregation . . . plus our future role in the community.

Each ministry team has also held numerous meetings and either formulated or updated goals and objectives for their department. Each team made great progress toward their goals; however, we have concluded that these efforts are not enough.

Let me tell you why . . .

In recent years there have been changes that have altered our congregational life and our relationship with the community. The completion of the addition to our church building has enabled us to provide new programs that reach out to the surrounding community, but there have also been a series of changes in our staff.

Like all mainline churches, we also face a tight financial period, and our membership numbers—despite some great new members joining—are not increasing when you consider the loss of some members that are retiring and moving out of state.

In light of these factors, we have concluded that we need to evaluate the direction our congregation should take in the future—and that an overall assessment of who and what we are and where we are going would help [your church name] grow in ministry and continue to be a healthy, active congregation.

We have decided that the best results could be obtained using a dedicated team and guidance from an expert coach.

In the meantime, know that we are *not* asking for financial support of this "assessment."

We *are* asking that you participate in the process, as we believe it is important we reenergize our church and update our long-term mission and vision statements and goals.

To assure that our church grows in ministry and continues to be a healthy, active congregation, a long-term planning project has been authorized by the Administrative Council. We will work on a Ministry Action Plan (MAP, for short) which is a structured, objective process coached by an expert Guided Process Servant (i.e., coach) provided to us at the suggestion of our conference staff. The team will lead the church in determining, by objective observation, what our key issues are for the next three to five years. This structured process will result in a MAP with goals and mileposts and a means of follow up to be recommended to the Administrative Council for implementation.

The team members are [names of members of the team] along with team leader, [name].

Input from everyone in the congregation is being sought by the team. A survey which the team hopes will be filled out by all members of the church is available this morning, as well as on our website. Please place the surveys in the box provided in the Welcome Center. Additional comments can be sent to our team leader by email [provide address]. We will update the congregation periodically on our progress. The target for completion of this project is [date].

Commissioning Liturgy for the *Roadmap to Renewal* Leadership Team

Dear Friends, you have been called by God and chosen for the special responsibility of visioning ministry. This ministry is a blessing and a serious responsibility. It will require the use of the gifts God has given you as you lead the congregation in reflection on its ministry in the community and in the world. In love we thank you for accepting your obligation and challenge you to offer your best to the Lord, to this team and to our mutual ministry. As you carry out the tasks that will require your time and energy, we urge you to call on the spiritual resources that God alone provides.

Today we commission [name each member of the team].

To the team members:

As you stand in the midst of the congregation and in the presence of God, will you do all in your power to be responsible to the task for which you have been chosen?

We will.

To the congregation:

Dear Friends in Faith, give thanks for these who stand before you. Will you do all you can to assist and encourage them in the responsibilities to which they have been called, giving them your cooperation, your counsel and your prayers?

We will.

Let us pray:

Gracious and eternal God, pour out your blessings upon these your servants who have been given this particular ministry of visioning for your church. Let their work, on behalf of the church that they love and to which they are committed, be guided by your powerful presence. Grant them grace to give themselves wholeheartedly in your service. Keep before them the example of our Lord, who did not think first of himself, but gave himself for us all. Guide them in their work. Reward their faithfulness with the knowledge that through them your purposes for the church are accomplished. Through your Spirit, inspire the whole congregation to be faithful and encouraging participants in this time of looking forward to the end that the witness of your people in the community and the world will be strengthened. We pray in the name of all that is holy and which brings life in all the abundance that we have seen in Jesus of Nazareth.

Amen.

Congregation Values Survey[1]

Select the top priority as 1 and rank the others 2 through 5:
Our church's primary concern should be:

☐ Charitable work   ☐ The spiritual needs of our members

☐ Members helping each other   ☐ Ministry to children and young people

☐ Teaching God's Word

Choose 5 items below that are MOST IMPORTANT to you and rank them 1 to 5 in order of priority as above:

☐ Administration   ☐ Adult ministry / education
(finances, building, etc.)

☐ Counseling / pastoral care   ☐ Discipleship

☐ Fellowship   ☐ Music ministry

☐ Outreach to the community/   ☐ Planning and setting goals
welcoming all

☐ Prayer   ☐ Small groups

☐ Sunday School   ☐ Training / equipping members to use
their gifts

☐ Welcoming new attendees   ☐ World Missions

☐ Worship

What should we stop doing?

What should we start doing?

1. This survey was put together by the leadership team of the Bishop Janes United Methodist Church in Basking Ridge, New Jersey, as they worked through the *Roadmap to Renewal* process. We thank them for permission to reproduce the survey here.

What should we continue doing?

The following questions relate to your personal view in regard to the church and its ministry. In response to the following statements, please circle the number corresponding to your opinion.

	Strongly Agree	Agree	Disagree	Strongly Disagree
I want our congregation to grow in size and bring new people.	1	2	3	4
Our church should be open to innovation and change.	1	2	3	4
I would prefer slow and steady change rather than rapid and progressive change.	1	2	3	4
I would rather see the church accept things as they come instead of planning and setting goals.	1	2	3	4
We should be more concerned with the needs of the community around us than the needs of our own members.	1	2	3	4
At church, my privacy is more important to me than intimacy.	1	2	3	4
We should have different styles of services.	1	2	3	4
We should have services at different times.	1	2	3	4
Lay people should be involved in the church's ministry.	1	2	3	4
We have the right programs in place for young families.	1	2	3	4
We have the right programs in place for teens and young adults.	1	2	3	4
We have the right programs in place for single people.	1	2	3	4
We have the right programs in place for seniors.	1	2	3	4
We have a good music program.	1	2	3	4

Age: 20 or under _____   21–40 _____   41–60 _____   61+_____

Gender (M/F): _____   Married or Single (M/S) _____

Ages of children in household:
Boys: ____, ____, ____, ____; Girls ____, ____, ____, ____

Others in my household have submitted a survey (Y/N): _____

Additional comments and concerns:

Name (optional): _____

Bibliography

Barna, George, and David Kinnaman, eds. *Churchless: Understanding Today's Unchurched and How to Connect with Them.* Carol Stream, IL: Tyndale, 2014.

Baughman, Michael, ed. *Flipping Church: How Successful Church Planters Are Turning Conventional Wisdom Upside-Down.* Nashville: Discipleship Resources, 2016.

Bishop, Paul. "*Lumen Gentium* (Dogmatic Constitution on the Church)." In *The Documents of Vatican II*, edited by Walter M. Abbott. New York: Herder & Herder, 1966.

Bonhoeffer, Dietrich. *Life Together; Prayerbook of the Bible.* Translated by Daniel Bloesch and James H. Burtness. Dietrich Bonhoeffer Works 5. Minneapolis: Fortress, 1996.

Breen, Mike, and Steve Cockram. *Building a Discipling Culture: How to Release a Missional Movement by Discipling People Like Jesus Did.* Pawleys Island, SC: 3D Ministries, 2011.

Bultmann, Rudolf. *The History of the Synoptic Tradition.* Translated by John Marsh. Rev. ed. Peabody, MA: Hendrickson, 1998.

Cole, Neil. *Organic Church: Growing Faith Where Life Happens.* San Francisco: Jossey-Bass, 2005.

Damián, Juan, ed. *Carta de Evangelización.* Montevideo: CLAI, 1979.

———. *Unidos.* Montevideo: CLAI, 1983.

Dietterich, Inagrace T., and Mike McCoy. "Sign, Foretaste, and Instrument." Chicago: Center for Parish Development, 1999.

Estock, Beth Ann, and Paul Nixon. *Weird Church: Welcome to the Twenty-First Century.* Cleveland: Pilgrim, 2016.

Fowl, Stephen E., and L. Gregory Jones. *Reading in Communion: Scripture and Ethics in Christian Life.* Grand Rapids: Eerdmans, 1991.

Fowler, James W. *Stages of Faith: The Psychology of Human Development.* San Francisco: Harper & Row, 1981.

Frazier, William. "The Church as Sign." In *The Church as Sign*, edited by William J. Richardson, 1–13. Maryknoll, NY: Maryknoll, 1968.

133

Hagiya, Grant. *Spiritual Kaizen: How to Become a Better Church Leader.* Nashville: Abingdon, 2013.

Harkness, Georgia. *Understanding the Christian Faith.* Nashville: Abingdon, 1974.

Hauerwas, Stanley, and William H. Willimon. *Resident Aliens: Life in the Christian Colony.* Nashville: Abingdon, 1989.

Job, Reuben P. *Three Simple Rules: A Wesleyan Way of Living.* Nashville: Abingdon, 2007.

Johnson, Paul. *A History of Christianity:* New York: Touchstone, 1995.

Jones, E. Stanley. *Is the Kingdom of God Realism?* New York: Abingdon-Cokesbury, 1940.

Kelsey, Morton T. *Companions on the Inner Way: The Art of Spiritual Guidance.* New York: Crossroad, 1983.

Kinnaman, David, and Gabe Lyons. *unChristian: What a New Generation Really Thinks about Christianity . . . and Why It Matters.* Grand Rapids: Baker, 2007.

Logan Robert E., and Tara Miller. *From Followers to Leaders: The Path of Leadership Development in the Local Church.* St. Charles, IL: ChurchSmart, 2007.

Maynard, Phil. *Readiness 360 Online Survey.* http://readiness360.org.

Miller, Craig Kennet. *Next Church.Now: Creating New Faith Communities.* Nashville: Discipleship Resources, 2003.

Mundell, E. J. "U.N. Seeks to Curb World's Traffic Deaths." *HealthDay News,* April 1, 2008. http://abcnews.go.com/Health/Healthday/story?id=4567253.

Nouwen, Henri J. M. *Clowning in Rome: Reflections on Solitude, Celibacy, Prayer, and Contemplation.* Garden City, NY: Image, 1979.

Ruffle, Douglas. *A Missionary Mindset: What Church Leaders Need to Know to Reach Their Community—Lessons from E. Stanley Jones.* Nashville: Discipleship Resources, 2016.

Schnase, Robert C. *Seven Levers: Missional Strategies for Conferences.* Nashville: Abingdon, 2014.

Sweet, Leonard. *The Gospel according to Starbucks: Living with a Grande Passion.* Colorado Springs: WaterBrook, 2007.

United Methodist Church. *The Book of Discipline of the United Methodist Church.* Nashville: United Methodist Publishing House, 2012.

———. *The Faith We Sing.* Nashville: Abingdon, 2001.

Weems, Lovett H. "Leadership for Reaching Emerging Generations." *Circuit Rider,* March/April 2006, 6.

World Council of Churches. *The Nature and Mission of the Church: A Stage on the Way to a Common Statement.* Faith and Order Paper 198. Geneva: WCC, 2005.

Wuthnow, Robert. *After the Baby Boomers: How Twenty- and Thirty-Somethings Are Shaping the Future of American Religion.* Princeton: Princeton University Press, 2007.